What
not
to write

A guide to the
dos and don'ts of good English

TALISMAN

© Kay Sayce 2007, 2009, 2010

ISBN 9780955279805

Published by
Talisman Publishing Pte Ltd
Singapore
Printed & bound by Bell & Bain Ltd., Glasgow

Written by: Kay Sayce
Edited by: Peter Joyce
Designed by: Anita Mangan
Illustrated by: Sarah Murchison

£8.54

DEDICATION
To my father, for showing me the beauty of written English,
and to my lovely and amazing daughters, Emma and Clare,
for their support in this venture

Contents

T.S. Eliot commended a world

…where every word is at home,
Taking its place to support the others,
The word neither diffident nor ostentatious,
An easy commerce of the old and the new,
The common word exact without vulgarity,
The formal word precise but not pedantic,
The complete consort dancing together.

Introduction

Believe it or not, someone in an office somewhere wrote this:

> As we endeavour to reach the one million pound level in sales, we intend to still remain highly focused by following our corporate strategy as follows:

- achieve excellence in all core competencies by developing and continually improving operational processes, systems, and controls

- grow the company and profitability through effective mission-oriented sales and marketing strategies whilst capitalizing on profitable new product, market and geographical opportunities

- pursue acquisition and investment windows to add and diversify growth and earnings potential

- manage gross margin, operating expenses, and asset employment carefully

- secure and maintain synergetic and trusting relationships with leading suppliers who devote significant resources to innovative product development

- nurture a passion for customer satisfaction

- maintain a superior work environment to attract and retain skilled, motivated and pro-active people.

The person who wrote this took more than a hundred words, many of them meaningless, to say: "We plan to be a well-run, profitable company."

If you work at a desk you're probably a writer. It might not be what you'd call yourself, but it is likely to be a big part of what you do every day. So you're entitled to call yourself a writer. A writer of e-mails. A writer of letters. A writer of minutes, reports, briefs, essays or articles, or perhaps of proposals, papers or press releases.

It is likely that you haven't been trained how to prepare these documents. You've just picked it up along the way by looking at how the people around you write, using the words and phrases they use, assuming that how you're expressing yourself is acceptable. But you don't know. No one has told you what the ingredients of good writing are. Grammar lessons are a dim or non-existent memory. Punctuation has always been a bit of a blur; there seems to be a fairly random approach to placing a comma or an apostrophe, and no one has ever enlightened you about the use of colons and semi-colons, or perhaps even what they are. Spelling is a bit hit-or-miss, but you now have that wonderful invention, the spell-checker, so it's simply a case of watching out for those wavy red lines.

You go along with the new long words and complicated phrases that come across your desk or via your computer. Often, you're not sure what they mean, but you want to feel part of things, so you decide to use them too. No one has told you that much of it is pretentious jargon and, like the excerpt opening this Introduction, simply adds to the mass of gobbledygook that now clutters so much workplace writing.

You're so busy that you seldom have time to plan what you are going to write, what points you need to make or in what order to make them, let alone the time to write more than one draft. Usually you just start writing, get it all down, check for those wavy red lines and press the 'SEND' button.

And do you really think about your readers? They might have to wade knee-deep through mangled grammar, random punctuation, meaningless verbiage, worn-out metaphors, toe-curling clichés, confused messages and, all in all, an uninspiring use of the English language.

But perhaps this is not you at all. Perhaps you do have a grasp of grammar, a dislike for bureaucratese, a fondness for simple words and uncomplicated sentences and a desire to produce functional writing that moves seamlessly and engagingly from point to point and enlightens your reader.

Whoever you are, if writing is part of your everyday life, this book is for you.

For those with a precarious understanding of what to write and what not to write, it will put you on the right path and make you want to find out more. For those of you who simply want to sharpen the skills you already have, it will help you do that and more. And both groups will find that, with this book close at hand, the task of writing will be easier and more enjoyable.

Using the book

The book takes you through the dos and don'ts of writing good English, from A to Z. It begins with the use of 'a' or 'an' before a noun and it ends with 'zero-sum game', a particularly unpleasant example of jargon.

It answers those questions you might hear one person asking another in an office, such as:

Is it 'a hotel' or 'an hotel'?
Do you spell 'judg(e)ment' with or without an 'e'?
How does American-English differ from British-English?
Do you write 'Yours truly' or 'Yours sincerely'?
What are split infinitives, and should you avoid them?
It's website? Its website? Where do you put the apostrophe?
What's an acronym?
What happens when you have brackets inside brackets?
Do you use capital letters for 'secretary-general'?
Is a semi-colon like a comma?
Do you know when to use 'that' or 'which'?
Is it 'between you and me' or 'between you and I'?

The entries in the A to Z all have examples of what to write and what not to write. You'll spot these examples easily because they are in bold and are preceded by the symbol ☼.

The Index is comprehensive. If you can't find what you're looking for in the A to Z entries, the Index will tell you where to look.

For example, you want to know what an ampersand is, but 'ampersand' is not one of the headings under 'A'. So go to the Index and it will direct you to 'abbreviations and contractions', where you'll find information about ampersands. Similarly, if you're not sure whether to write 'he/she', 's/he' or 'he or she', go to the Index and it will direct you to 'sexist writing'.

If you're not sure about the meaning of a term used in the A to Z, the Index will direct you to an entry that explains that term.

For example, if you're not sure what 'sentence case' and 'title case' mean, the Index will direct you to 'capital letters', where you'll find the answer. Similarly, if you're unclear about the difference between a 'clause' and a 'phrase', the Index will direct you to Appendix 1.

The Appendices provide useful background material. Appendix 1 is a guide to basic grammar, where there are short, clear explanations of terms, with examples. The Appendices also contain a checklist of points to think about when you start writing something, tips for those of you who do page-layout work and a short list of other books you might find useful.

When you look at these other books, you'll notice that there are some aspects of written English where the approach differs. There is much debate, for example, about whether or not to split infinitives, when you put a comma before 'and', when to use hyphens and dashes, and whether or not to abandon the use of 'shall' after a pronoun and always use 'will' instead. Whatever approaches you adopt, the important point is to be consistent in applying them.

The most important point of all, however, is that English is an extraordinary language – fluid, flexible and dynamic, the product of many languages and able to constantly adapt itself to changing circumstances. Writing English should be a pleasure, not least because it offers so many ways of expressing the same idea. There *are* rules and conventions, as this book shows; use them not to impose a rigidity on your writing but rather as a foundation on which to build the confidence to explore the richness and versatility of the language and to put your message across, whatever it is, in a way that will capture readers' attention.

Do enjoy dipping into these pages and do remember, always, that simple English is the best English.

An A to Z of good English

The entries in this A to Z contain examples of what to write and what not to write. You'll spot these examples easily because they are in bold, preceded by the symbol ☼ .

If you can't find what you're looking for among the A to Z headings, refer to the Index and it will tell you which entry heading to look under.

a / an

'A' and 'an' come before a noun. Whether you put 'a' or 'an' depends on whether the noun begins with a *vowel sound*, not necessarily a *vowel letter* (i.e., it depends on pronunciation, not spelling). ☼ **an effort, an honour, an MA, an SOS message, a European conference, a hotel, a union, a university.** 'A' and 'an' are known as 'indefinite articles'; 'the' is called the 'definite article'.

See also: Appendix 1 under 'determiner'

abbreviations and contractions
(Feb., Fig., Prof., edn, Revd, St, you're)

There is a difference between an *abbreviation* and a *contraction:*

- An abbreviation is the first part of a word and it ends with a full stop. ☼ **'et al.', 'etc.', 'Feb.', 'Fig.', 'Prof.' abbreviated from 'et alii', 'et cetera', 'February', 'Figure' and 'Professor'.** It also refers to sets of initials (*see* acronyms).

- A contraction telescopes a word, keeping the last letter, and it does not end with a full stop. ☼ 'edn', 'Revd', 'Mt', 'St' and 'you're' contracted from 'edition', 'Reverend', 'Mount', 'Saint' and 'you are'.

ACADEMIC QUALIFICATIONS: Abbreviations of academic qualifications use a mixture of upper and lower case; they don't have full stops (and are therefore exceptions to the rule above). ☼ **BA, BSc, BPhil, MA, MSc, PhD, PhDs.** (For more on upper and lower case *see* capital letters.)

AMPERSANDS: Avoid using an ampersand (&) instead of 'and', except where it is always used in an abbreviation or an official name or title. ☼ **C. Brown and A. Jones (*not* C. Brown & A. Jones), *Pride and Prejudice* (*not* Pride & Prejudice), R&D (for 'research and development'), R&B (for 'rhythm and blues'), Fortnum & Mason plc.**

BIOLOGICAL CLASSIFICATION: When you first mention the name of a genus (e.g., *Musa*, the genus or biological group to which bananas belong), put it in its full form; after that, abbreviate it, using only the first letter of the genus. ☼ **The cultivation of *Musa sapientum* and *M. textilis* is common here.** Don't abbreviate a genus name, however, when (i) it starts a sentence or (ii) several genera with the same initial letter are mentioned in the same piece. Use the abbreviation 'sp.' after a genus name when you're referring to one species; for more than one species, use 'spp.' ☼ **Several *Musa* spp. have been reclassified.**

COMPASS POINTS: If you abbreviate compass points, use capital letters. ☼ **SE, NW.** Unless you're writing a technical document, however, it's better not to abbreviate compass points. There is a hyphen between unabbreviated compass points. ☼ **Frankfurt is about 380 kilometres north-west of Munich (*not* 380 kilometres NW of Munich).**

DATES AND TIME: Use 'a.m.' and 'p.m.', always in lower case. Don't shorten 'year' to 'yr' except in diagrams and tables.

Write the abbreviations of days and months thus: ☼ **Sun. Mon. Tue. Wed. Thur. Fri. Sat.; Jan. Feb. Mar. Apr. May June July Aug. Sept. Oct. Nov. Dec.** (For more on lower case *see* capital letters.)

INFORMAL LANGUAGE: Don't, isn't, won't, I'm, you've, they're – the use of such contractions depends on what you are writing. Don't use them if you are writing formal documents. But if you're writing something that needs a light tone (e.g., informal letter, instruction manual, press release, set of guidelines), it's fine to use, for example, 'don't' instead of 'do not', or 'they're' instead of 'they are'. If in doubt, it's better not to use contractions.

MEASUREMENTS OF AREA, DATA STORAGE, DISTANCE, TEMPERATURE, TIME, VOLUME AND WEIGHT: Use the standard abbreviations for units of measurement that follow a number (*see* Box 13). ☼ **2 cm** (*not* 2 cm. or 2 cms), **100 ha, 5 g, 3 km, 60° C, 4 min, 5 t.** When you're expressing a measurement less precisely, don't use the abbreviation. ☼ **The house is several kilometres from the river** (*not* The house is several km from the river). **They land several tonnes of fish daily.**

PERSONAL TITLES: When you're shortening personal titles, use a full stop if the title's last letter is not the same as the last letter in the shortened version. If the letters are the same, there is no full stop. ☼ **Dr, Mr, Mrs, Prof., Revd, Rt Hon.**

MISCELLANEOUS:

- Be careful with the punctuation for the abbreviations of 'for example' ('e.g.' from *exempli gratia*) and 'that is' ('i.e.' from *id est*). There is a comma after the second full stop. ☼ **She covered several issues (e.g., recruitment, training and promotion). The paper was too short (i.e., one side only)** (*not* 'i.e. one side only'; this would read as 'that is one side only' which, without the pause after 'is', does not have the same meaning).

- In bibliographies, the shortened versions of 'editor' and 'editors' are 'ed.' and 'eds'. For 'edition' (as in '3rd edition') and 'volume', they are 'edn' and 'vol.' The abbreviations 'p.' and 'pp.' stand for 'page' and 'pages', respectively.

See also: acronyms; Appendix 3 under 'word breaks'; Box 1; company names; countries and regions

---

Box 1   ROMAN HANGOVER

ABBREVIATION	WORD	MEANING
c./ca	*circa*	about; approximately
cf.	*confer*	compare with
c.v.	*curriculum vitae*	course of life (summary of education and career information)[1]
e.g.	*exempli gratia*	for example
et al.	*et alii*	and others
et seq.	*et sequens*	and the following
etc.	*et cetera*	and the rest
ibid.	*ibidem*	in the same place (referring to a publication mentioned earlier)
i.e.	*id est*	that is
NB	*nota bene*	note well
op. cit.	*opere citato*	work cited previously
q.v.[1]	*quod vide*	look elsewhere
ult.	*ultimo*	of the previous month
viz.	*videlicet*	namely
vs	*versus*	against; as opposed to

1   It is more common now to see 'c.v.' written as 'CV' and q.v. written as 'qv'.

-able / -eable / -ible

Whether a word ends in -able, -eable or -ible usually depends on the origin of that word. If you're not sure whether to write, for example, 'accessible' or 'accessable', 'favourable' or 'favourible' and 'tracable' or 'traceable', refer to the dictionary (where you will find ☼ **accessible, favourable, traceable**).

about / around

When you're giving an estimate of something, it's best to use 'about' rather than 'around'. ☼ **There were about 50 people there (*not* around 50). It was about 4 p.m. when the meeting ended (*not* around 4 p.m.).** When the meaning is fairly broad, though, it's acceptable to use 'around'. ☼ **The change happened around the middle of the century.** If in doubt, use 'about'.

accents
(à ç é ñ ô ü)

Examples of accents include: acute (é), cedilla (ç), circumflex (ô), grave (à), umlaut (ü) and tilde (ñ). Foreign words that are commonly used in English, but lack an accurate English equivalent, should keep the accents they have in the original language if this affects their pronunciation. ☼ **café, cliché, façade (these words would be pronounced differently if they did not have an accent); elite, naive (*not* 'élite' or 'naïve' because these words would not be pronounced differently without an accent).**

You should keep the accents in the names of foreign organisations and institutions, whether or not the name appears in capital letters. ☼ **Institut national d'études démographiques, INSTITUT NATIONAL D'ÉTUDES DÉMOGRAPHIQUES.**

acronyms
(ABTA, NATO, OPEC)

There is a difference between an *acronym* and an *abbreviation:*

- An acronym is a set of initials representing the name or title of something and making a word. In most cases, an acronym doesn't have 'the' before it. ☼ **ABTA, AIDS, NATO, NICE, OPEC, RIBA. NATO's offices are in Poirot Square in Brussels. The training provided by ABTA is comprehensive.**

- When a set of initials doesn't make a word and (usually) needs 'the' before it, it is an abbreviation. ☼ **BBC, CBI, EU, IMF, UN, USA, WTO. The IMF is based in Washington. Membership of the EU has expanded.** (*See* abbreviations and contractions.)

The full form of an acronym or abbreviation for an organisation is always in title case, not sentence case. ☼ **World Trade Organisation (***not* **World trade organisation).** Some organisations use lower case in their acronyms; always use what an organisation itself uses. ☼ **Anzac, Oxfam.** (For more on lower case, sentence case and title case *see* capital letters.)

Acronyms and abbreviations can also be initials representing a common phrase or entity. ☼ **non-governmental organisation (NGO), human resources (HR).** Don't use full stops in acronyms and abbreviations. ☼ **CBI (***not* **C.B.I.).** The plurals of acronyms and abbreviations have a lower case 's' (with *no* apostrophe). ☼ **NGOs (***not* **NGO's).** (*See* Box 15.)

When you first mention an acronym or abbreviation in a document, you should put the full form, followed by the abbreviation or acronym in brackets. After that, use only the abbreviation or acronym. ☼ **The Association of British Travel Agents (ABTA) was among the bodies represented**

as discussed...

as per our telephonic discussion

at the seminar, although **ABTA** staff seldom attended such meetings. Some abbreviations and acronyms are so familiar that there's no need to use the full form. ☼ **AIDS, BBC, UK, USA.**

When the name of an institution or organisation is in a foreign language and there is no official English equivalent, use the foreign name, followed in brackets by the acronym and the translation of the foreign name. ☼ **Fédération des unions de producteurs (FUPRO; Federation of Farmers' Unions).** In French, the names of organisations are always in sentence case. (For more on sentence case *see* capital letters.)

Don't repeat the last word of an acronym or abbreviation. ☼ **The last word of WTO is 'Organisation', so don't write 'the WTO organisation'. Similarly, write 'HIV',** *not* **'HIV virus', because the 'V' in the abbreviation stands for 'virus'.**

Box 2 ACCENTUATE THE POSITIVE

It is easier to understand sentences that are positive rather than negative.

> *A negative sentence:*
> Members of staff other than those recruited before 2000 are not eligible for the bonus.

> *Its positive version:*
> Only members of staff recruited before 2000 are eligible for the bonus.

When you do have to write something negative, it's often best to choose a single word rather than a phrase. For example:

does not have	lacks
does not include	excludes
not able	unable
not accept	reject
not around	absent
not certain	uncertain
not many	few
not often	rarely; seldom
not the same	different

There are some instances where a negative phrase or sentence has more punch than the positive version. For example, *What To Write* would be a less catchy book title than *What Not To Write*.

active / passive voice

Verbs have two voices. When the subject of a sentence is doing something, you're using the active voice; when the subject is being acted upon, you're using the passive voice. Try to use the passive voice sparingly. If you use it too much, your writing will seem heavy and pedantic. Using the active voice creates lighter and more readable text. ✿ **John Smith opened the meeting (*not* The meeting was opened by John Smith). We have read your report (*not* Your report has been read).**

Sometimes, however, for irony or dramatic effect, the passive is more appropriate. ☼ 'Keith Richards opened the seminar on skin care' lacks the impact of 'The seminar on skin care was opened by Keith Richards.'

addresses

Always write an address as it appears on an organisation's letterhead or website, with no rearrangement or translation. ☼ If, on a letterhead or website, the post code comes before the name of the town, don't put the post code after the name of the town because you're more used to seeing it that way. It's fine to translate the name of the country, though. ☼ If the addressee's letterhead has 'Belgique', you could write 'Belgium' instead.

☼ Carens-Transports
Avenue Jean XXI, 3
B–1899 Rixensart
Belgium

Telephone and fax numbers should start with the country code prefaced by '+'; separate the sets of numbers by spaces, not hyphens.

☼ Carens-Transports, Avenue Jean XXI, 3, B–1899 Rixensart, Belgium. Telephone: +32 2 757 7681; fax: +32 2 757 7682; e-mail: info@cts.co.be; website: www.cts.com

See also: abbreviations and contractions; names of people

adjectives, adverbs and compound terms
(smart, smartly, smartly dressed)

An adjective is a word that describes a noun. ☼ **A *smart* person.** An adverb describes a verb. ☼ **This person is** *smartly* dressed. A compound term consists of two or more linked words that describe a noun. ☼ **A smartly dressed person.** (For more on adjectives, adverbs, nouns and verbs *see* Appendix 1.)

Use adjectives sparingly. The use of too many adjectives is a sign of poor writing. Your key words – the nouns and verbs – should be strong enough to convey your message.

Place adverbs as you do when speaking. ☼ **He went boldly (*not* He boldly went). She greatly admired him.**

Don't put a hyphen between an adverb and an adjective if the adverb ends in '-ly'. ☼ **Genetically modified organism (*not* genetically-modified organism); newly built premises (*not* newly-built premises).**

Many common compound terms need a hyphen to avoid ambiguity. ☼ **A cross-cutting issue (without a hyphen between 'cross' and 'cutting', this could mean an angry issue, wielding a knife); a little-known politician (without a hyphen between 'little' and 'known', this means a short politician who is well known).** Other examples include ☼ **Bristol-based director, capacity-building project, clear-cut procedure, first-class service, long-term plan, out-of-town trader, part-time worker, question-and-answer service, small-scale enterprise, well-established agency, 18th-century house.**

See also: American-English / British-English; Appendix 2; Box 3; Box 8; comma; hyphens and dashes; numbers; long term / short term

almost / nearly

'Nearly' refers to distance. It's not the same as 'almost', which usually refers to amount. ☼ **We have driven almost 50 kilometres, so we are nearly there.**

Box 3   THREE FACES OF THE ADJECTIVE

For most adjectives, you add -er and -est to the end for the comparative and the superlative, respectively, as in the first six adjectives below. But there are exceptions.

ADJECTIVE	COMPARATIVE	SUPERLATIVE
big	bigger	biggest
cold	colder	coldest
high	higher	highest
low	lower	lowest
old	older	oldest
wise	wiser	wisest
common	commoner *or* more common	commonest *or* most common
narrow	narrower *or* more narrow	narrowest *or* most narrow
pleasant	pleasanter *or* more pleasant	pleasantest *or* most pleasant
acceptable	more acceptable	most acceptable
beautiful	more beautiful	most beautiful
serious	more serious	most serious
intelligent	more intelligent	most intelligent
bad	worse	worst
good	better	best
little	less	least
many	more	most

alphabetical order

When you're writing a list of things, such as a list of countries, put them in alphabetical order unless you have a good reason not to do so (in which case, give the reason). ☼ **The seminar** participants came from Germany, Italy, Portugal, Spain and the UK. The rapporteurs were C. Dickens, G. Grass and W. Yeats. The main speakers were, in order of appearance: J. Zapatero, A. Blair, R. Prodi and A. Merckel.

See also: bibliographies and reference lists

American-English / British-English

American-English words and expressions are creeping into British-English, not least because of the internet. Americans have their own valid and effective ways of expressing themselves, and it's worth noting that their language style is not necessarily new. The word 'gotten', for example, goes back to Shakespearian times, and the American habit of dropping the '-ly' from adverbs (he passed the ball *quick*

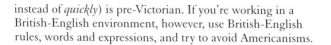

instead of *quickly*) is pre-Victorian. If you're working in a British-English environment, however, use British-English rules, words and expressions, and try to avoid Americanisms.

The differences between British-English and American-English spellings affect mainly words ending in -ce, -ement, -our and -re. ☼ **offence (*American-English [AE]:* offense), acknowledgement (*[AE]:* acknowledgment), labour (*AE:* labor), centre (*AE:* center).**

Differences in expressions often relate to the use of verbs. ☼ **Appeal against a decision (*AE:* appeal a decision); meet someone (*AE:* meet with someone).** American-English uses some nouns also as verbs. Common examples are 'impact', 'author' and 'pressure'. In British-English, these are nouns, not verbs. ☼ **She was the author of the report (*AE:* She authored the report). The change had an impact on staff (*AE:* The change impacted on staff).** In American-English 'progress' is often used as a verb to mean 'move something along', but it should not be used this way in British-English. ☼ **Work on the new building progressed (*AE:* They progressed work on the new building).** In American-English 'grow' is often used as a verb in relation to companies; in British-English you 'grow' plants, but you 'develop' or 'expand' companies. ☼ **Grow sugar cane. Grow roses. Expand the company (*AE:* Grow the company).**

American-English tends to drop hyphens after some prefixes. In British-English this should be avoided. ☼ **anti-malarial (*AE:* antimalarial), by-product (*AE:* byproduct), co-publication (*AE:* copublication), non-governmental (*AE:* nongovernmental), post-harvest (*AE:* postharvest).**

For examples of differences between British-English and American-English spellings and expressions *see* Box 4.

See also: Box 5; comma; dates and time; different; hyphens and dashes; -ise / ize; learnt / learned; spelling

Box 4 TOMA(R)TO vs TOMA(Y)TO

Here are some examples of differences between British-English and American-English spellings and expressions.

BRITISH-ENGLISH	AMERICAN-ENGLISH
Spellings	
aesthetic	esthetic
ageing	aging
ambience	ambiance
amoeba	ameba
analogue	analog
analyse	analyze
archaeology	archeology
artefact	artifact
catalogue	catalog
cheque	check
colour	color
cosy	cozy
defence	defense
encyclopaedia	encyclopedia
enrolment	enrollment
favour	favor
fibre	fiber
fulfil	fulfill
gauge	gage
jewellery	jewelry
judgement[1]	judgment
labelled	labeled
learnt (verb)	learned
licence (noun)	license
manoeuvre	maneuver
mollusc	mollusk
mould	mold
offence	offense
programme[2]	program
rivalled	rivaled
skilful	skillful
sulphur	sulfur
travelling	traveling
tyre	tire

BRITISH-ENGLISH	AMERICAN-ENGLISH
Expressions	
a rise (in salary)	a raise (in salary)
appeal against a decision	appeal a decision
at the weekend	on the weekend
autocue	teleprompter
closing down	closing out
current account	checking account
different from	different than
estate agent	realtor
foot the bill	bankroll
fortnight	two weeks
engaged tone	busy signal
ground floor	first floor
have an impact	impact
hire purchase	installment plan[3]
inside	inside of
is the author of	authored
maths	math
meet	meet with
outside	outside of
post code	zip code
proved[4]	proven
put pressure on	pressure
superannuation	retirement fund
timetable	schedule
transport	transportation
write to (someone)	write (someone)

In British-English, until recently a 'billion' meant a 'million million' (12 noughts), not a 'thousand million', as in American-English. A 'trillion' meant a 'million billion' (18 noughts), not a 'million million'. But British-English has now aligned itself to American-English usage.

1   But in British-English write 'judgment' when referring to a judge's or court's formal ruling (this distinguishes a 'judge's judgment' from a 'personal judgement' which judges cannot express in their official capacity).
2   But write 'program' in British-English when referring to a computer program or when the word is part of an official name.
3   In British-English, write 'instalment'.
4   But write 'proven' in British-English when using it as an adjective.

amid / among / between

Use 'amid' and 'among' rather than 'amidst' and 'amongst', which are a throwback to earlier times. 'Between' refers to two items; when referring to more than two items, use 'among'. ☼ **The correspondence between the manager and the bank was published. The information was shared among all members of the network (*not* between all members of the network).**

If you're putting a pronoun after 'between', it should be an object pronoun (me, him, her, us, them), not a subject pronoun (I, he, she, we, they). ☼ **There is little difference between you and him (*not* There is little difference between you and he). Between you and me, I'm not happy about this (*not* Between you and I, I'm not happy about this).** In *The Merchant of Venice*, Shakespeare wrote, "All debts are cleared between you and I." This wasn't necessarily a mistake because the rule about writing 'between you and me' wasn't written until the 1860s. (For more on pronouns *see* Appendix 1.)

Don't put 'each' or 'or' after 'between'. ☼ **There was a pause between the shots (*not* There was a pause between each shot). She had to choose between promotion and leaving the company (*not* She had to choose between promotion or leaving the company).**

See also: dates and time; numbers

amount / number

Use 'amount' before something that can't be counted, but use 'number' before something that can be counted. ☼ **The amount of paper used was limited. The amount of food was inadequate. The number of pages ran into hundreds. A large number of people attended the meeting.**

See also: almost / nearly; fewer / less

apostrophe

The wrong use of the apostrophe (') has become so widespread that there is now an Apostrophe Protection Society.

An apostrophe with an 's' ('s) denotes the possessive (by 'possessive' we mean something or someone belonging to something or someone).

For singular nouns, including those that end in 's', you put the apostrophe at the end of the noun, with an 's' *after* it ('s). ☼ **accountant's office, CD's label, cat's whiskers, Clare's book, everyone's friend, town's shops.** Names and other nouns ending in 's' often cause confusion. Write them as you would pronounce them. ☼ **In speech you'd say ' James's car' (*not* 'James' car'), Paris's airports, Ross's number.** If you're referring to an item that two nouns share, put the apostrophe after the second noun. ☼ **Matthew and Emma's house.**

For plural nouns ending in 's', you use the apostrophe without the 's' after it. ☼ **doctors' organisations, Joneses' house, CDs' labels, 5 years' experience, Americans' point of view, peoples' survival** (as in 'the survival of peoples', but if you mean 'the survival of people', you put 'people's survival').

An apostrophe also denotes contractions or missing letters. ☼ **I'd (I would), he'll (he will), don't (do not), it's (it is).** The word 'it' causes problems because the contraction of 'it is' – it's – looks like the possessive. ☼ **It's going to rain (meaning 'It is going to rain'). It's late (meaning 'It is late').** But the possessive of 'it' is 'its' (just as the possessive for 'him' is 'his' and for 'her' is 'hers'). ☼ **The agency launched its new website.**

Don't use apostrophes in words that are simply plurals. ☼ **1990s (*not* 1990's), dos and don'ts (*not* do's and don't's), whys and wherefores (*not* why's and wherefore's), successes** (*not* success's), twos and threes, MPs, CVs, two dry Aprils, the three Rs.

See also: abbreviations and contractions; acronyms; Appendix 2; Box 15

as

'As' has many meanings and can occur many times in a sentence. You should try to avoid it where possible by replacing it with words with the same meaning, such as 'because' and 'for'. ☼ **We postponed the meeting because several people were ill (*not* We postponed the meeting as several people were ill).**

You could also try rephrasing a sentence in which 'as' occurs too often. ☼ **'As we are aware, the manager has been seen as committed as well as hard working, but his commitment is now being questioned as he has started spending more time away from the office.'** This could be rewritten thus: **'The manager has been committed and hard working, but the time he is now spending away from the office calls this commitment into question.'**

because

Don't use 'because' in a sentence after the words 'reason' or 'reason why'. It's unnecessary repetition. ☼ **The reason they missed the train was that the car broke down (*not* The reason they missed the train was because the car broke down). They missed the train because the car broke down (*not* The reason why they missed the train was because the car broke down).**

It's regarded as poor style to use 'because' at the beginning of a sentence.

See also: as; due to

before / previous

'Before' should always be followed by a noun, so don't put it at the end of a sentence. Use 'previous' instead. ☼ **The trainees had applied in the previous year (*not* The trainees had applied the year before).**

beside / besides

'Beside' means 'next to' or 'alongside'. 'Besides' means 'in addition to' or 'apart from'. ☼ **He stood beside the lectern. Besides the reports, there were posters and brochures.**

bi-annual / biennial / bi-monthly / bi-weekly

'Bi-annual' and 'biennial' both mean 'once every 2 years'. Confusingly, bi-annual also means 'twice a year'. Similarly, 'bi-monthly' and 'bi-weekly' mean 'twice a month/week *and* 'every 2 months/weeks'. So avoid using these terms unless their meaning is clear from the context. Instead, use phrases such as 'twice a week' and 'every 2 years'.

bibliographies and reference lists

This entry is of interest mainly to authors of books, academic papers and lengthy reports.

A 'Reference list' or 'References' contains only those works (books, papers, etc.) mentioned in a text; it should provide details on all of them. A 'Bibliography' can list more than only those works mentioned in a text. A 'Select bibliography' (or 'Further reading' list) contains works not necessarily mentioned in the text, but thought important by the author and intended for further reading. (In the rest of this entry, the term 'bibliography' is used to cover all these forms.)

There are many rules about compiling bibliographies, too many to cover here; for more detail, consult the *Oxford Guide to Style* (*see* Appendix 4). Here, we provide simple guidelines on what information to put in a bibliography and how to present it.

An item in a bibliography is generally arranged in the following order:

* name(s) of author(s) or editor(s), with the surname first, then the initials (don't put titles, such as Dr, Mrs or Professor); if no author or editor, put the publisher's name

* after editors' names put '(ed.)' if there is only one editor or '(eds)' if more than one

* date of publication

* this information is followed by:

    – FOR PUBLISHED WORKS (e.g., books): title in italics and title case; then edition (edn) and volume (vol.) numbers in brackets, if applicable; then name of publisher(s) and place of publication (town/city *and* country). (For more on sentence and title case *see* capital letters.)

    – FOR REPORTS, PAPERS AND BOOK CHAPTERS: title in sentence case within single quotation marks and not in italics; then (if published in a book) *'In'* in italics followed by names of author(s) or editor(s); then book title in italics, followed by the order of information for published works (*see above*).

    – FOR PAPERS AND ARTICLES IN JOURNALS AND MAGAZINES: title in sentence case within single quotation marks and not in italics; then name of journal or magazine, in italics; then volume number; then issue number (in brackets, unless there is no volume number) and the page numbers. The word *'Journal of'* can be abbreviated to *'J.'*.

Sometimes you'll see variations of this arrangement. For example, the date is put in brackets, the initials for the first author precede the surname, or the place of publication precedes the name of the publisher. If you choose to follow such variations, that's fine, so long as you apply them consistently throughout the bibliography.

Always put the items in a bibliography in alphabetical order (unless the bibliography is divided into categories, in which case the items in each category should be in alphabetical order). Works by a single author come before those by the author in collaboration with other authors; if there is more than one work by the same single author, list them chronologically. When there are two or more items published by the same authors (single or multiple) in the same year, they should be labelled 'a', 'b', etc. after the date.

✿ Fowler, H.W. 2001. *A Dictionary of Modern English Usage.* (8th edn). Oxford University Press, Oxford, UK.

James, P.L., Smith, A. and Williams, P.V. 1998. 'Uncertainty and monetary theory.' *In* James, P. (ed.) *The New Economic Horizon.* Random House, New York, USA.

Smith, V. and Jones, S. 1997a. 'Evaluating information channels.' *J. Information Society* 15 (23): 47–59.

Smith, V. and Jones, S. 1997b. 'IT and the layperson.' *Information Networking* 8: 5–17.

When citing works in text, put the surname and publication date in brackets; if there are three or more authors, give only the first surname, followed by 'et al.' ✿ **Using the examples above, the citations would be written: (Fowler 2001), (James et al. 1998) and (Smith and Jones 1997a).**

See also: abbreviations and contractions; capital letters; colon; et al.; italics; names of people

Box 5 BEGINNINGS AND ENDINGS

The main part of a noun is called the root. To many nouns you can add a
prefix (before the root) or a suffix (after the root) to modify its meaning.
Most prefixes and suffixes derive from Greek and Latin words.

cycle – *bi*cycle – cycl*ist*   ROOT = cycle; PREFIX = bi- ; SUFFIX = -ist
danger – *en*danger – danger*ous*   ROOT = danger; PREFIX = en- ; SUFFIX = -ous

COMMON PREFIXES	MEANING	EXAMPLE
ad-	to	adhere
ante-	before	antecedent
anti-	opposite	antidote
auto-	self	autobiography
bi-	two	bicycle
con-	with	congratulate
de-	from; down	depart
dis-	not; opposite	disable
en-	bring into	endanger
ex-	out	expel
inter-	among; between	international
intra-	within	intranet
macro-	large	macro-economics
micro-	small	microscope
mis-	bad	miscarriage
mono-	single	monopoly
neo-	new	neo-liberal
pan-	all	pandemic
poly-	many	polygamous
post-	after	postnatal
pre-	before	preview
re-	again	restart
sub-	under	submarine
trans-	across	transatlantic

COMMON SUFFIXES	MEANING	EXAMPLE
-al	relating to	maternal
-algia	pain	neuralgia
-dom	state of	freedom
-ess	female	goddess
-graph	written; drawn	autograph
-ic	relating to	poetic
-ile	state of	juvenile
-ism	system of; theory of	atheism
-ist	one who practices	cyclist
-ography	written about; representation of	biography
-ology	study of	biology
-ous	state of	dangerous
-phile	likes; loves	anglophile
-phobe	dislikes; hates	technophobe
-port	carry	export
-ular	relating to	cellular
-vert	turn	invert

When attaching 'over' and 'under' to a word, don't use hyphens.
☼ overdone (*not* over-done) and undervalued (*not* under-valued).

both

Don't use 'both' if you're referring to more than two. ☼ **Both the manager and her new deputy were there** (*not* **Both the manager, her new deputy and the customer were there**).

Where 'both' occurs with a preposition (e.g., 'in' or 'at'), put the preposition first. ☼ **It was in both *The Guardian* and *The Times*** (*not* **It was both in *The Guardian* and *The Times***). (For more on prepositions *see* Appendix 1.)

brackets

Remember that every opening bracket must be followed at some point by a closing bracket.

If you need to put text into brackets, use curved brackets ( ). These are also known as 'parentheses'. If text within the curved brackets also needs to go into brackets, use square brackets [ ]. ☼ **The participants included people from Europe (France [18], Wales [24]) and South-East Asia (Singapore [12], Thailand [4], Vietnam [7]).**

You can also use square brackets to add something to a quotation, by way of explanation. The square brackets show that your addition is not part of the original quotation. ☼ **She said, "He advised [the journalists] to use only on-the-record material."**

Also use square brackets to insert '[sic]' in a quotation to denote a mistake in the original that you need to point out. ☼ **The letter noted that "the project in Bulgaria, near Budapest [sic], had ended."**

See also: acronyms; bibliographies and reference lists; comma; hyphens and dashes

brief / quick

'Brief' means 'short'. 'Quick' means 'fast', but it is often used incorrectly instead of 'brief'. ☼ **The appendices contain brief notes (*not* The appendices contain quick notes).**

capital letters

Capital letters are also called 'caps' or 'upper case'. Letters not in capitals are 'lower case'.

'Title case' means that the first letter of all words in a set of words is a capital letter, apart from prepositions (e.g., 'by', 'for', 'on' and 'with') and the definite and indefinite articles ('the', 'a' and 'an'). (For more on articles and prepositions *see* Appendix 1.)

'Sentence case' means that capital letters in a set of words are used as they would be in a normal sentence. The first word has an initial capital letter, but the rest of the words do not, unless they are proper nouns. (For more on proper nouns *see* Appendix 1.)

PUBLICATIONS AND MEETINGS: Use title case for the titles of publications (books, journals, etc.) and publication series. ☼ **In the Project Planner series, the book entitled** *Participatory Learning* **is very popular.** Use sentence case for titles of meetings and for texts that are part of a publication (such as an article in a magazine, a paper in a report or a chapter in a book). ☼ **The CBI organised a seminar on**

31

'Literacy in the workplace' last year. In *The Project Workout*, the second chapter on 'Defining the project cycle: The way forward' is particularly good.

COMPASS POINTS: Use capital letters when the compass point is part of a proper name or politically defined region.
☼ **Central America, the Far East, Middle East, North Korea, South-East Asia, the West (in the political context).** Use lower case when referring to geographical areas.
☼ **south-east India, the north-eastern part of China, western Sudan.** (*See* abbreviations and contractions.)

GEOGRAPHICAL AND URBAN FEATURES: Use title case when these features are part of a proper name. ☼ **Black Forest, Mexico City, Mount Everest, River Danube, Trafalgar Square.** Otherwise, use lower case. ☼ **savanna, highlands, the delta region.**

HISTORICAL PERIODS: Use title case for defined historical periods. ☼ **Cold War, Bronze Age, First World War, Renaissance.** Use lower case for less well-defined periods.
☼ **the colonial era, the post-independence era, the space age.**

INSTITUTIONS, ORGANISATIONS AND DEPARTMENTS: Use title case. ☼ **Cambridge University, Department of the Environment, European Commission, Institute of Fiscal Studies, Ministry of Trade, Roman Catholic Church.** If you're referring to an organisation or group in a shortened form after using it in its full form, use lower case. ☼ **The ABTA Advisory Committee met in the morning, but some committee members were absent** (*not* **The ABTA Advisory Committee met in the morning, but some Committee members were absent**).

PERSONAL TITLES, RANKS AND OFFICE HOLDERS: When a title precedes someone's name, it begins with a capital letter.
☼ **Colonel Qadaffi, IBM Chairman Louis V. Gerstner Jr, President Bush, Queen Beatrice, Secretary-General Kofi Annan.** When a title is not part of the name, it is in lower

case. ☼ **The president, Mr Bush, spoke. The president of Afghanistan arrived. The secretary-general of the United Nations flew to Brussels. The IBM chairman, Louis V. Gerstner Jr, was there.**

THE NET: When the internet was still fairly new, many of the words associated with it began with a capital letter. It is now more common to see these words in lower case. ☼ **net, internet, website.**

TREATIES, CONVENTIONS, AGREEMENTS AND ACTS: Use title case. ☼ **Bill of Rights, Maastricht Treaty, UN Human Rights Convention.**

See also: abbreviations and contractions; acronyms; Appendix 3 under 'tables'; bibliographies and reference lists; Box 10; Box 19; colon; countries and regions; currencies; quotations

captions

Try to keep captions (for illustrations such as diagrams, line drawings, photos and graphs) as short as possible, but make sure that they answer the questions that an illustration might raise (e.g., Who are the people in the photo? Where are they? What are they doing? What is the event?).

If you're writing several captions, make sure they're all in the same style (e.g., all full sentences, or all phrases, but not a mixture of the two). Generally, captions are not full sentences. Don't end a caption with a full stop, whether or not it's a full sentence. (For more on phrases and sentences *see* Appendix 1.)

☼ **Discussions during the NATO sub-committee meeting on Bosnia, showing (left to right): Peter Ashdown, Douglas Owen and Gavrilo Grahovac**

See also: Appendix 3 under 'illustrations', 'lines and fonts' and 'spacing'; italics

Box 6   THE BANE OF BUREAUCRATESE

The drive to promote simple English has made great progress in recent years, but there are still people in the business and professional communities and among bureaucrats who try to make communication as murky as possible.

On the left are some words and phrases that repeatedly offend. On the right are their better, simpler versions.

along the lines of	like
am in a position to	can
announced	said
appreciate your advice on	please let me know
approximately	about
as per our telephonic discussion	as discussed
as regards	about; concerning
as to whether	whether
at all times	always
at an early date	soon
at such time as	when
at the present time	now
at your earliest convenience	soon
commence	begin; start
communicate with us	write to me; let me know
considerable period of time	long time
consume	eat
due to the fact that	because
elucidate	explain
endeavour	try
fullest possible extent	fully
furnish me with	let me have
implement	carry out
in a satisfactory manner	well; satisfactorily
in accordance with	by; with
in close proximity to	near
in connection with	about; concerning
in regard to	about; concerning
in the absence of	without
in the event that	if
in the majority of instances	mostly; usually
in view of the fact that	as; because

it is our opinion that	we think; we believe
kindly	please
manufacture	make
notwithstanding the fact that	although
permit	let
prior to	before
purchase	buy
reside	live
subsequent to	after
sufficient	enough
terminate	end
the majority of	most
the question as to	whether
utilise	use
with reference to	about; concerning
with regard to	about; concerning

collective nouns
(committee, crowd, government, team)

It's often difficult to decide whether verbs should be singular or plural when they're linked to a group (collective noun). If the focus is on the group as a single unit, use singular verbs; if it's on individual members of the group, use plural verbs. If you're still not sure, read the sentence aloud, replacing the collective noun with 'it' or 'they' to see which one sounds correct. ✿ **The committee (it) was elected. The committee (they) have been arguing about the minutes. The staff (they) were all busy. The United Nations (it) has decided. The couple (they) have left the wedding reception. The Seychelles (it) has a new president. The headquarters (they) are in Geneva.** (For more on verbs *see* Appendix 1.)

For some words ending in '-ics', use the singular form of the verb unless the word is preceded by 'the'. ✿ **Economics is not my favourite subject. The logistics are complicated.**

colon

The colon (:) has two main functions. One is to separate two ideas. ☼ **He wanted only one thing: promotion. One man dominates English cricket: 'Freddie' Flintoff. Development work is much more than a job: it is a contribution to improving the lives of people less fortunate than you are.** When you use a colon in a publication title, the first word after the colon has a capital letter. ☼ ***The Fifth Discipline: The Art and Practice of the Learning Organisation.*** This also applies to headings and subheadings. ☼ **Improving distribution systems: Case studies in France and the Netherlands.** If the text before a colon is in italics, italicise the colon too. ☼ ***Stage 1:* The building blocks of writing.**

The other main function of a colon is to introduce a list. Here, you can use it to replace such terms as 'namely', 'for example', 'therefore' and 'as follows'. Don't add a dash after the colon (:–). ☼ **The paper was divided into three parts: the background, the main argument and the conclusion.** This could be written as a bulleted list:

☼　The paper was divided into three parts:
  • the background
  • the main argument
  • the conclusion.

You can also use a colon to introduce a quotation. ☼ **In his book on English usage, H.W. Fowler writes:**

> **The English-speaking world might be divided into (1) those who neither know nor care what a split infinitive is; (2) those who do not know, but care very much; (3) those who know and condemn; (4) those who know and approve; and (5) those who know and distinguish.**

Use a colon to separate the two figures in a ratio. ✿ **The ratio of staff to passengers is about 1:400. Sausage meat is a 70:30 mixture of meat and fat.**

In bibliographies, use a colon before the page numbers in a journal reference. ✿ *Journal of Plant Sciences* **5 (32): 114–17.**

See also: bibliographies and reference lists; lists

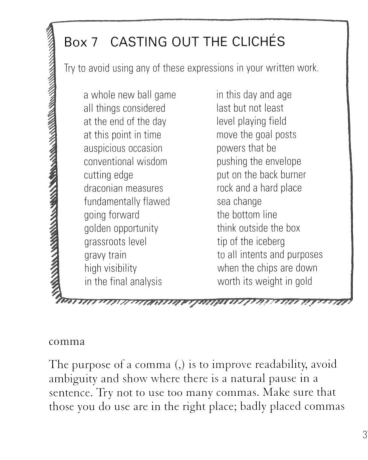

Box 7   CASTING OUT THE CLICHÉS

Try to avoid using any of these expressions in your written work.

a whole new ball game	in this day and age
all things considered	last but not least
at the end of the day	level playing field
at this point in time	move the goal posts
auspicious occasion	powers that be
conventional wisdom	pushing the envelope
cutting edge	put on the back burner
draconian measures	rock and a hard place
fundamentally flawed	sea change
going forward	the bottom line
golden opportunity	think outside the box
grassroots level	tip of the iceberg
gravy train	to all intents and purposes
high visibility	when the chips are down
in the final analysis	worth its weight in gold

comma

The purpose of a comma (,) is to improve readability, avoid ambiguity and show where there is a natural pause in a sentence. Try not to use too many commas. Make sure that those you do use are in the right place; badly placed commas can alter the sense of a sentence. ☼ 'Managers, who are aloof, should not be promoted' does not mean the same as 'Managers who are aloof should not be promoted' (The first one implies that all managers are aloof and therefore should not be promoted, whereas the second one is talking about not promoting a certain type of manager – aloof ones). ABTA's 15th annual seminar, on airline food, was held in Brussels (*not* 'ABTA's 15th annual seminar on airline food was held in Brussels'; this implies that 'airline food' has been the subject of every one of ABTA's 15 annual seminars).

A comma before the 'and' in a list (series) of words is known as a 'series comma'. It is common in American-English, but not in British-English. ☼ **The committee members were drawn from Wales, Scotland and the West Midlands** (*not* **from Wales, Scotland, and the West Midlands**). **The shop sold apples, pears and oranges** (*not* **apples, pears, and oranges.**

Don't use the series comma in British-English unless:

- the meaning of the sentence would be ambiguous if you didn't. ☼ **Among the guests were representatives from Grenada, Jamaica, and Trinidad and Tobago** (the comma separates Trinidad and Tobago, which is one country, from the other two countries).

- the last item in a list of three or more would lose its impact without a comma. ☼ **Mad, bad, and dangerous to know** (the series comma gives the necessary emphasis to 'dangerous to know').

- you're using an extension phrase (*see opposite page*).

Don't use commas when writing dates. ☼ **22 August 2004** (*not* **22 August, 2004**).

Use commas instead of brackets or dashes to separate information. If this makes a sentence difficult to understand, however, then by all means use brackets or dashes. ☼ **Instead of 'Project evaluation should start at the implementation, some would say the planning, or even the conceptual, stage' it would be better to write 'Project evaluation should start at the implementation (some would say the planning, or even the conceptual) stage' or 'Project evaluation should start at the implementation – some would say the planning, or even the conceptual – stage.'**

Use a comma:

- to separate an independent clause from a dependent clause. ☼ **If it rains in January, the maize crop will survive.** (For more on clauses and phrases *see* Appendix 1.)

- after an opening phrase. ☼ **In the 1990s, the focus moved towards 'action learning'. Organised in Exeter, the seminar was well attended.**

- before and after adjectival phrases or clauses. ☼ **Some agencies, most of which had connections with Jersey, pushed for higher air fares.**

- before and after appositives (an appositive is a noun that follows another noun to identify or clarify its meaning). ☼ **The chairperson, Jane Mundy, sat down.**

- between adjectives that come before a noun. ☼ **It is a simple, fast and cheap method of communication.**

- to separate unrelated numbers. ☼ **In May 2006, 162 people visited the new headquarters.**

- before an extension phrase (e.g., ..., and so forth; ..., and the like; ..., and so on; ..., etc.). ☼ **Let's take buckets, spades, umbrellas and sandals, etc. The guests included actors, comedians, writers, and so on.**

See also: abbreviations and contractions; Box 8; dates and time; however; hyphens and dashes; numbers; quotations; semi-colon; that / which

Box 8 AVOIDING THE DOUBLE MEANING

Ambiguity usually occurs when you don't use commas properly or when the order of clauses and phrases in a sentence is muddled. It can have some amusing results, as that master of ambiguity, Groucho Marx, recognised. "I once shot an elephant in my pyjamas," he said in the film *Animal Crackers,* adding, "How he got into my pyjamas I'll never know."

Here are some other examples.

"This conflict becomes apparent when the protagonist is forced into a corner between chapters three and four."

"No one was injured in the blast, which was attributed to a build-up of gas by one town official."

"The singer will talk about her husband John who was killed in an interview with Barbara Williams."

"The summary of information contains totals of the number of students broken down by sex, marital status and age."

"One witness told the panel that she had seen sexual intercourse taking place between two parked cars in front of her house."

"The narrator describes what is tearing the community apart in a long passage."

"Drunk gets nine months in violin case"

commence

Try to avoid using this rather starchy word. Use more common words with the same meaning, such as 'start' or 'begin'.

See also: Box 6

company names

You should follow a company's own spelling and punctuation of its name. When you first mention the name, use the full version. ☿ **Unilever Ltd was among the first companies to invest there. Other companies followed in the 1950s, but few did as well as Unilever.** Use ampersands (&) and contractions only if the company uses them. ☿ **Fortnum & Mason, Warner Bros.**

See also: abbreviations and contractions

compare

After the word 'compare' put 'with' (*not* 'to') if differences are being described. ☿ **The output from factory A was poor compared with the output from factory B.** Only when 'compare' is used to stress similarity, rather than difference, should you put 'to'. ☿ **"Shall I compare thee to a summer's day?"**

comprise / compose / consist

The meanings of these words are similar. They all relate to the parts of something that make up a whole. 'Comprise' means 'is composed of' (so don't put 'of' after it). 'Consist' should always be followed by 'of' and never by 'in'. ☿ **The group was composed of artists and copywriters. The group comprised artists and copywriters. The group consisted of artists and copywriters.**

concept

The word 'concept' is often used when what is meant is simply 'idea' or 'notion'. Use 'concept' only for something complex, such as 'Freud's concept of sexuality' or 'Hawking's concept of time', or for something that is clearly an elaboration of an idea or notion.

copyright

In published works (e.g., books), you usually find the copyright information on the imprint page (the back of the title page, also called the 'title verso') or on the back cover. In magazines and newspapers, it's usually in the colophon (a box or column containing the publication's production details). The copyright information consists of the copyright symbol (©) followed by the name of the copyright owner and the date of copyright.

The copyright period for published works is the life of the author and for 70 years after the author's death. You need permission from copyright owners to quote their text if a quotation exceeds 400 words.

Don't forget to acknowledge the source of all illustrations in a publication. A common way of doing this is to place, alongside each illustration, a copyright symbol and the name of the copyright owner.

See also: Appendix 3 under 'illustrations' and 'order'

countries and regions

When you're writing about countries, use the pronoun 'it' rather than 'he', 'him', 'she' or 'her'. ☼ **India is emerging as an economic power. It has become a major player in the global economy (*not* She has become a major player).** (For more on pronouns *see* Appendix 1.)

Use 'country' rather than 'nation' or 'State', except in clearly political contexts. ☼ **The initiative involved six countries in** the Pacific region. **Representatives of the five nations on the Security Council were present. The effect of State withdrawal from providing health services has been significant.** 'State' has a capital letter to differentiate it from 'state' as in 'announce' or the 'condition' of something.

You don't need to spell out UK (United Kingdom) or USA (United States of America). Use the abbreviation 'UK' rather than 'Britain' or 'Great Britain', which refer only to England, Scotland and Wales, excluding Northern Ireland. Don't use 'England' when you mean the UK.

Use 'USA' (*not* America). Use 'North America' only when you're referring to the whole continent, including Canada and Mexico. It's acceptable, however, to write 'American companies' rather than 'USA companies' or 'US companies'.

Here are some more country and regional names to look out for:

- Congo (the smaller country, capital city Brazzaville)
- Democratic Republic of Congo (the larger country, capital city Kinshasa; the country is often referred to as the 'DRC')
- Côte d'Ivoire (Ivorians prefer this to 'Ivory Coast')
- Latin America (*not* South America)
- Lebanon (*not* the Lebanon)
- the Netherlands (*not* Holland, which officially refers to only two provinces of the country)
- Myanmar (*not* Burma)
- Sudan (*not* the Sudan)
- the Philippines (*not* Philippines)
- Yemen (*not* the Yemen).

Use 'European Union' (EU) unless you're referring specifically to the European Economic Community (EEC), which existed from 1957 to the late 1960s, or to the European Community (EC), which existed from the 1960s to 1995.

See also: capital letters

criteria

The word 'criteria' is plural. The singular form is 'criterion'.
☼ **The criterion for entry is a degree. The criteria for entry are a degree and an interest in current affairs.**

currencies

When you're referring to currencies, you should specify the country as well as the monetary unit, unless this is clear from the context. Currency names do not have capital letters.
☼ **UK pounds, US dollars, Swiss francs, Indian rupees, Ugandan shillings.**

Use currency symbols, not words, when you're writing specific amounts. ☼ **€20, US$20, £20, Rs20 (*not* 20 euros, 20 USD, 20 US dollars, 20 GBP, 20 pounds, 20 rupees).** Don't put a space between the symbol and the numeral.

When linking two amounts, don't repeat the symbol or 'million' or 'billion'. ☼ **£50–75 (*not* £50–£75); £5–6 million (*not* £5 million–6 million or £5 million–£6 million).**

See also: hyphens and dashes; fewer / less; numbers

data

The word 'data' is plural. The singular form is 'datum'.
☼ **The data are reliable (*not* The data is reliable).**

dates and time

The order for a date: day month year (with no commas).
☼ **25 August 2004 (*not* 25th August, 2004 or August 25th, 2004).** In American-English, the month precedes the day, hence the common term '9/11' referring to 11 September 2001.

Also put:

- 1990s (*not* 1990's)

- 21st century (*not* 21st Century or twenty-first century)

- from 12 to 14 June, between 12 and 14 June (*not* from 12–14 June or between 12–14 June)

- the period 1994–97 (*not* the period from 1994–97 or the period 1994–1997)

- the period 2001–02 (*not* the period from 2001–02 or the period 2001–2002)

- the period 1997–2002 (*not* the period from 1997–2002 or the period 1997–02)

- 10 a.m. (*not* 10 am or 10 o'clock), 4.15 p.m. (*not* 4.15 pm or a quarter past four). Use the 24-hour clock (e.g., 10.00 h or 16.15 h) only when you're writing for an audience that works with it. Remember that 12 a.m. is midnight and 12 p.m. is midday; to avoid confusion, it's best to write '12 midnight' or simply 'midnight' and '12 noon' or 'noon'.

Be careful when referring to a past date from the standpoint of the present. You can't be sure exactly when people will read your work. ☼ **They moved in 2003 (*not* 'They moved 2 years ago.' Someone reading this in 2007 would assume that the move took place in 2005).** Similarly, don't use terms that will become out of date (e.g., 'currently', 'last year', 'soon' and 'recently') unless you're sure they won't be misunderstood.

See also: abbreviations and contractions; Appendix 3 under 'word breaks'; bibliographies; comma; fewer / less; last / past; numbers; superscript

different

Use 'different from', not 'different than' (the latter is American-English) or 'different to'. Where possible, use 'differ' rather than 'different'; it's simpler. ☼ **The procedures differ from those used in previous years (*rather than* The procedures are different from those used in previous years).**

See also: Box 4; Box 9

do

'Do' is often used incorrectly after 'used to'. ☼ **In the sentence 'We don't have the space we used to', the verb here would be 'have' (as in 'used to have'). So 'We don't have the space we used to do' would be incorrect.**

double negative

If you use a double negative, the meaning of your sentence will often be the opposite of what you intend because the second negative (e.g., 'no') cancels out the first negative (e.g., didn't). ☼ **They didn't want any food (*not* 'They didn't want no food.' This means 'They wanted food').**

Box 9   WASTED WORDS

ACTUAL, ACTUALLY: Seldom necessary, unless you want to stress the contrast
between something that is real and something that is hypothetical or
not real. ☼ We saw the house in which he was born (*not* We
saw the actual house in which he was born). She doesn't like
chairing the meetings (*not* She doesn't actually like chairing the
meetings).

BASIC, BASICALLY: Often used unnecessarily. ☼ The idea is to attract
people from leading firms (*not* The basic idea is to attract people
from leading firms). She's rather lazy (*not* She's basically rather
lazy).

CONCRETE: Avoid, unless you *do* mean the building material. A fact is no more
a fact if it is called 'a concrete fact'. Try no adjective at all, or use a
meaningful one. ☼ The reports provided examples of policy
changes (*not* The reports provided concrete examples of policy
changes). We offer practical solutions (*not* We offer concrete
solutions).

DIFFERENT: Often used in a redundant way. Where a distinction does need
to be made, try 'various' or 'several' instead. ☼ People came from
various countries (*not* Different people came from different
countries). The designs were based on three styles (*not* The
designs were based on three different styles). He visited several
countries (*not* He visited different countries).

EXIST: Seldom necessary. It's usually better to delete or replace it with 'is'
or 'are'. ☼ The gap between rich and poor is wide (*not* The
gap that exists between rich and poor is wide). There are
several training centres in Stroud (*not* There exist several
training centres in Stroud).

FIND, FOUND, AVAILABLE: Often used when all you need is 'is', 'are', 'has' or
'have'. ☼ The information is on the website; the site also has
useful links to other projects (*not* The information can be found
on the website; also available on the site are useful links to
other projects).

GET, GOT: Often used unnecessarily after 'have' or instead of the verb 'to be' (e.g., after 'was' and 'were'). ☼ I have eyesight problems (*not* I have got eyesight problems). I have to go abroad (*not* I have got to go abroad). He was stopped at the border (*not* He got stopped at the border).

LITERALLY: Often used as padding or for emphasis, frequently resulting in ludicrous statements. ☼ She was so angry she hit the roof (*not* She was so angry she literally hit the roof). He's flooded with work (*not* He's literally flooded with work).

LOCATED: Usually best deleted or replaced by the simpler words 'find' or 'found'. ☼ Brussels is in Belgium (*not* Brussels is located in Belgium). The house is 1 mile north of the M25 (*not* The house is located 1 mile north of the M25). The missing report was found in the storeroom (*not* The missing report was located in the storeroom).

REAL: Seldom adds anything meaningful. ☼ There is a lack of interest in the subject (*not* There is a real lack of interest in the subject).

SAME: Often used in a redundant way. ☼ On the day that they were due to start, he resigned (*not* On the same day that they were due to start, he resigned).

THE FACT THAT: Avoid; 'that' will usually do just as well. ☼ Given that there was no meeting, she stayed at home (*not* Given the fact that there was no meeting). He was unaware that the figures were old (*not* He was unaware of the fact that the figures were old).

VERY, HIGHLY: Seldom add anything worthwhile and can often be replaced by something better. ☼ 'The food was good' hardly differs from 'The food was very good.' It would be more meaningful to write 'The food was tasty and well presented.' The trainees watched some practical demonstrations (*not* The trainees watched some highly practical demonstrations').

You can use a double negative deliberately to make a positive statement, but avoid this if it sounds cumbersome or could confuse the reader. ☼ **It is likely (*better than* It is not unlikely). The show was impressive (*not* The show was not unimpressive).**

due to

Don't use 'due to' instead of 'because of'. Use 'due to' only when it means 'owed to', 'attributable to' or 'scheduled to'. ☼ **She arrived late because of a delayed train (*not* She arrived late due to a delayed train). A month's salary was due to the secretary. The campaign's success was due to good team work. The books are due to arrive soon.**

e-

The prefix 'e-' stands for 'electronic'. It's often written without the hyphen, but that could lead to problems in the fast-evolving world of information technology, so it's better to retain the hyphen. ☼ **e-mail, e-forum and (who knows) e-elections (*not* email, eforum, eelections).**

effectively / in effect

These don't mean the same thing. 'Effectively' means 'with effect' or 'with impact'. 'In effect' means 'more or less' or 'had the same effect'. ☼ **The software was effectively promoted. The meeting ended, in effect, when drinks were served.**

either...or / neither...nor

Use these when referring to only two options (not three or more). Don't use 'or' with 'neither', or 'nor' with 'either'.

Where 'either' or 'neither' occurs with a preposition (e.g., 'at', 'in', 'near' or 'on'), put the preposition first. ☼ **It was in either *The Guardian* or *The Times* (*not* It was either in *The Guardian* or *The Times*).** (For more on prepositions *see* Appendix 1.)

'Neither' should always be followed by a singular verb. ☼ **Neither of them likes working late (*not* Neither of them like working late).**

ellipses

An ellipsis (…) indicates omitted text. If you're using a quotation, for example, you might want to use only the first and last part of the quotation, not the part in between, but you need to indicate this middle part. You do this by using an ellipsis. ☼ **Look at the first paragraph under the entry on 'American-English / British-English'. If you want to quote only the first and last sentences of this paragraph, you'd put: "American-English words and expressions are creeping into British-English, not least because of the internet…If you're working in a British-English environment, however, use British-English rules, words and expressions, and try to avoid Americanisms."**

There is no space before or after an ellipsis.

Some purists add a fourth point if the omission comes at the end of a sentence (to denote a full stop), but this isn't necessary.

Ellipses can also indicate a deliberately unfinished sentence or a pause in speech. ☼ **The woman smiled, and yet…**

In a Word document you create an ellipsis by holding down the Control and Alt keys while pressing the Full Stop key (on an Apple Mac, press the Alt and Colon/Semi-Colon keys).

emotive and judgemental words

Try to avoid using terms that are emotive or suggest a partial stance (unless you do intend to be partial). ☼ **Population growth (*not* population explosion), serious disease outbreak (*not* a terrible disease outbreak).**

et al.

Until recently, people tended to put 'et al.' in italics, but now it is more common not to put it in italics. ☼ **There are more than 10,000 apple varieties (Smith et al. 2004) (*not* Smith *et al.* 2004).** The 'al.' is an abbreviation of *alii* and so you need a full stop after it.

See also: abbreviations and contractions; Box 1; italics

etc.

When you're introducing a list of items with a term that tells your reader that the list is not complete (e.g., 'including', 'such as', 'for example'), don't put 'etc.' at the end of the list. ☼ **The features on the website include commodity briefings (*not* The features on the website include commodity briefings, etc.). They export cereals such as wheat and barley (*not* They export cereals such as wheat and barley, etc.).**

Try to avoid using 'etc.' too much. When you do use it, remember that it is followed by a full stop because it is an abbreviation of *et cetera*.

Don't write 'and etc.' because 'etc.' already includes the word 'and' (*et cetera* means 'and other things').

See also: abbreviations and contractions; Box 1; comma

Box 10 GETTING E-MAILS RIGHT

Here are some guidelines for writing e-mails:

1   Before you do anything, ask yourself this: Is sending an e-mail necessary? Would my message be better conveyed by a phone call?

2   Having decided to send an e-mail, you need to decide whether to make it formal or informal. Informal e-mails can start with such words as 'Hi' or 'Hello', or have no opening salutation at all. With formal e-mails it's best to follow the usual letter-writing conventions (Dear…). (*See* letters.)

3   E-mails are regarded as more informal than business letters, but that doesn't mean that it's all right to use poor grammar in them or misspell words.

4   Using informal language is fine, as long as you're sure your recipient would not find it a problem. Contractions (I'd, you're, we've, they'll, etc.) give e-mails a light, informal touch. (*See* abbreviations and contractions.)

5   The main point about e-mails is that they are a fast form of communication, so they should be kept as short as possible. Put the key message of your e-mail up front and don't add unnecessary information.

6   It's also important to keep e-mails short because most people find it difficult reading great chunks of text on screen. They are more likely to read and act upon messages that are short and to the point.

7   If you have several subjects to cover, it might be best to put them in separate e-mails, not lumped together in one.

8   Keep paragraphs to three or four lines of text. Ensure that the text doesn't sprawl all the way across the screen.

9   Don't be tempted to use fancy fonts. They are difficult to read on the screen. Sans serif fonts such as Arial, Avant Garde and Verdana are best. (For more on fonts *see* Appendix 3 under 'lines and fonts'.)

10 Don't type the text in 'all caps' (capital letters). It's like shouting at the reader.

11 Check that the symbols you use in e-mails will appear as you intend them to. For example, the '£' symbol sometimes becomes '?' on transmission, which is off-putting for the reader.

12 Wait until you have written, checked and double-checked your e-mail before you key in the recipient's name. Hitting the 'SEND' button too early can have painful or embarrassing consequences.

exclamation mark

Use the exclamation mark (!) sparingly. Its use is justified only when someone is exclaiming, shouting or commanding. ☼ **Stand at ease! The woman shouted, "Go away!"** It's often used to indicate humour, but seldom effectively so.

farther / further

If in doubt, use further. Farther relates only to geographical distance. ☼ **She had a further request. Do we need to talk further? It's further to London than to Manchester. It's farther to London than to Manchester.**

fewer / less

When you have a plural noun describing items that can be counted, use 'fewer'. If it's a plural noun describing items that can't be counted, use 'less'. ☼ **Fewer books, fewer data, fewer people. Less work, less food, less coverage.** The exception is when 'less' is followed by 'than' and an amount of something (such as distance, time or money). ☼ **It's less than 3 metres. It takes less than an hour to get there. It costs less than £5.**

See also: more than / less than

first / firstly

There's much debate about whether you should write 'first' or 'firstly' ('second' or 'secondly', etc.). We recommend writing 'first'. ☼ **First (*not* Firstly), define the vision. Second, design the product. Third, formulate the marketing strategy.**

following / next

When you're referring to a particular moment, use 'following' if the sentence is in the past tense and use 'next' if it is in the present or future tense. ☼ **The book will be launched next week. In the following week, they launched the book (*not* In the next week, they launched the book).**

foreign terms

You should avoid using foreign words if there is an accurate English equivalent (but this doesn't apply to the foreign names of people, organisations, etc.). ☼ **Per person (*not* per capita), per year (*not* per annum).** When you do use a foreign word, put it in italics unless it has become commonly used. ☼ **She spoke *sotto voce*. The arrangements were rather ad hoc. The topics covered were, inter alia, human rights and water supplies. The café is on the corner.**

See also: Box 1; accents; acronyms; italics; names of people

former / latter

'Former' and 'latter' refer to one of only two (not one of three or more). ☼ **In the trials with wood and plastic, the former did well. (Here, 'former' refers to 'wood' and 'latter' refers to 'plastic'). In the trials with wood, plastic and bone, wood did well (*not* In the trials with wood, plastic and bone, the former did well).** If in doubt, it's best not to use 'former' and 'latter'.

full stop

Don't use full stops at the end of titles, headings and subheadings.

See also: abbreviations and contractions; acronyms; captions; ellipses; et al.; etc.; lists; names of people; quotations; semi-colon

hopefully

This is often used incorrectly. It means 'with hope' and should not be substituted for 'I hope', 'it is hoped', etc. ☼ **The hungry child walked hopefully towards the feeding station. Sales will improve, we hope, by July (*not* Hopefully, sales will improve by July).** The use of 'hopefully' in the incorrect sense, however, is now so widespread that this will probably become accepted usage.

however

The meaning of 'however', followed by a comma, differs from the meaning when there is no comma. If you're using 'however' to mean 'in spite of this', 'on the other hand' or 'nevertheless', you need a comma. If you're using it to mean 'no matter how', don't put a comma after it. ☼ **We've found a job for you in London. However, you might prefer to work in Birmingham (*not* However you might prefer to work in Birmingham). The situation, however, is not clear. However hard we tried, we couldn't get through.**

human resources

It's better to write 'staff', 'personnel' or 'people' than 'human resources', unless you are writing about various resources. ☼ **Staff development revolved around in-house training workshops. Among the constraints are limited financial resources and inadequate human resources.**

hyphens and dashes

The hyphen (-), the short dash (–) and the long dash (—) are used for different purposes.

In a Word document you create the short dash (also called an 'en rule' because it's the width of an 'n') by holding down the Alt key while pressing the Minus key on the numeric pad (on an Apple Mac, press the Alt and Hyphen keys). For the long dash (an 'em rule', the width of an 'm'), hold down the Control and Alt keys and press the Minus key on the numeric pad (on an Apple Mac, press the Alt, Shift and Hyphen keys).

The hyphen is used in four ways:

- within words (e.g., after a prefix or to show a word break). ☼ **neo-liberal, non-negotiable, pre-eminent.**

- between linked words (e.g., in compass points and compound terms). ☼ **south-east, private-sector investment, value-added goods, up-to-date records, 3-week holiday, 20-year-old house.**

- when there is a collision of vowels. ☼ **agro-ecology, co-operation, hydro-electricity, micro-organism, socio-economic.**

- to avoid confusion. ☼ **co-worker, re-creation, re-enact.**

The short dash is used to link numbers, as well as to link words that are separate entities (i.e., they don't make up a word, as hyphenated words do). ☼ **1914–18 war, £5–6 million, 2001–04 period, 2–5% of the goods, Blair–Bush approach, London–Paris–Berlin axis.**

The long dash is used, with a space on either side, to amplify or emphasise something. ☼ **Whether you walk or drive, you must be on time — it's important.** You can also use long dashes to show that the words between them should be read as if in brackets. ☼ **The addition of two new criteria — timeliness and presentation — was a good idea.** Try not to use long dashes more than once in a paragraph.

This conventional and rather archaic approach to the use of dashes is changing. Many leading publishers have abandoned the long dash and are using the short dash for both purposes. ☼ **London–Paris–Berlin axis. Whether you walk or drive, you must be on time – it's important. The addition of two new criteria – timeliness and presentation – was a good idea.** If you look through this book, you'll see that this is the approach that we use.

See also: abbreviations and contractions; addresses; adjectives, adverbs and compound terms; American-English / British-English; Appendix 3 under 'orphans and widows'; Box 5; colon; comma; e- ; lists; long term / short term; mid- ; numbers; self-

I / me / myself

Use 'I' before a verb, when it is the subject of a sentence. Use 'me' after a verb, when it is the object. ☼ **My colleague and I will be there** (*not* **My colleague and me will be there**). **Thanks for inviting my colleague and me** (*not* **Thanks for inviting my colleague and I**). If in doubt about whether to use 'I' or 'me', take away the other person (or people) and see how it sounds. ☼ **From 'My colleague and me will attend the meeting' take away 'My colleague and' and you are left with 'me', so the sentence would read 'Me will attend the meeting'**). (For more on sentences *see* Appendix 1.)

Don't use 'myself' as a variant of 'I' or 'me'. ☼ **Mary and I will be there** (*not* **Mary and myself will be there**). **She gave the reports to Jack and me** (*not* **She gave the reports to Jack and myself**). 'Myself', 'yourself', 'himself', 'herself', 'ourselves', 'yourselves' and 'themselves' should be used in only two ways. One is to emphasise the personal pronoun (e.g., I, you, he, she, we, they). ☼ **I myself do not subscribe to that opinion. He himself was absent, although he'd called the meeting.** The other use is when the personal pronoun is both the subject and object of the verb. ☼ **He pushed himself hard. They congratulated themselves on a job well done. She looked at herself in the mirror.** (For more on pronouns *see* Appendix 1.)

See also: amid / among / between

if / whether

These two words are not interchangeable. Use 'if' when there are no alternatives. Use 'whether' when there are alternatives (indicated by 'or'). ☼ **Let me know if you want to drive** (*not* **Let me know whether you want to drive**). **Let me know whether you want to drive or walk** (*not* **Let me know if you want to drive or walk**).

-ise / -ize

Style guides differ in their lists of words that should end in -ise / -yse and those that should end in -ize / -yze. Unless you're sure which it is (and/or know the Greek origin of the word you're using), it's best to use -ise / yse. ☼ **advertise (*not* advertize), advise (*not* advize), analyse (*not* analyze), compromise (*not* compromize), despise (*not* despize), exercise (*not* exercize), organisation (*not* organization), realise (*not* realize), sympathise (*not* sympathize).**

In American-English -ize / -yze is more common. This is not an 'Americanism', though; -ize / -yze has been used in English since the 16th century. For the official names of American institutions, use -ize / -yze. ☼ **American Rye Organization.**

italics

Use italics for:

- words and phrases in foreign languages, except for those that are now so familiar they don't need to be italicised. ☼ **ad hoc, apartheid, avant-garde, bona fide, café, coup d'état, et al., inter alia, vice versa. The *jojoba* is a type of desert shrub. She complained of having a *casse tête*.**

- titles of publications (e.g., books, newspapers, newsletters, journals, magazines). ☼ *Animal Farm, The Financial Times, Journal of Information Technology, Vogue.*

- names/titles of aircraft, artworks, CDs, films, plays, long poems (book length), musical compositions, radio and television programmes, and ships. ☼ *Enola Gay, Mona Lisa, The Dark Side of the Moon, Star Wars, Romeo and Juliet, The Ballad of Reading Gaol, Eroica* symphony, *The Archers, Big Brother,* HMS *Invincible.*

- emphasis. ☼ It's not *what* you do, but *how* you do it. Avoid using bold to emphasise something, if possible.

Don't use italics for:

- titles of book series, journal articles, chapter headings, papers, reports, poems (excluding book-length ones, *see above*), songs and unpublished material ('grey literature'). You should put all these titles between single quotation marks.

If the word, phrase or title that should go into italics is sitting in text that is already in italics (e.g., in a photo caption), then put that word, phrase or title in plain. ☼ *Anthony Brown, author of* The Blue Hills*, at the Savoy dinner*

See also: Appendix 3 under 'headings' and 'tables'; bibliographies and reference lists; colon; et al.; foreign terms

jargon, metaphors, clichés and hype

The English language is at its best when it is at its plainest and simplest. It's at its worst when weighed down with jargon, clichés and hype. All documents should be written in clear, simple English to ensure understanding, save time and create a good impression.

The word 'jargon' has two meanings. One is the technical language of a particular profession or discipline (e.g., economics, engineering, law, psychology). It's fine to use technobabble if you're sure your readers will understand it. The other meaning is the pretentious, verbose and often intimidating language that turns documents into meaningless gobbledygook. There is a good example of this on page 1. Among the 'jargon' words and phrases that have become common are ☼ **'actors' (instead of people), 'interface' (instead of 'border' or 'work with'), 'not unmindful' (instead of 'know') and 'oriented' (attached to almost everything, after a hyphen).** (*See* Box 6.)

A metaphor is a way of describing something in terms of something else to enhance the impact or image of what you're writing. ☼ **The news ignited her face. He inspected the food with a vulture's eye. The wind was scratching at the window. He shot down my argument.** Metaphors can be effective if used sparingly and carefully. But, as George Orwell noted, "there is a huge dump of worn-out metaphors which have lost all evocative power and are merely used because they save people the trouble of inventing phrases for themselves." The worst culprits are so overused that they become clichés. Clichés add nothing to your writing: avoid them. (*See* Boxes 7 and 11.)

We live in an age of hype. Like metaphors, there are more and more words that, from excessive use, have lost their power and become rather trite. ☼ **Instead of 'rise', 'fall', 'gain' and 'lose', people write 'surge', 'tumble', 'spiral' and 'crash' when often the context is not dramatic enough to warrant the use of such words.** The more accurate and appropriate the language, the more credible its message.

See also: Appendix 2; short words and phrases; synergy; zero-sum game

kind / sort / type

Avoid using 'kind of', 'sort of' and 'type of' unnecessarily. When you do use them, note that 'type' has a more formal,

Box 11   MIXED METAPHORS

A metaphor is a way of describing something in terms of something else to enhance the impact or image of the writing. (*See* jargon, metaphors, clichés and hype.)

A mixed metaphor occurs when you use two conflicting metaphors to describe something. So, rather than enhancing the impact or image of what you're writing, you confuse the reader.

> *For example:* 'The topic of child rearing is clouded in a sea of psychological terms.'

The metaphor is mixed because the images of *cloud* and *sea* don't match. The writer should have put:

> 'The topic of child rearing is drowned in a sea of psychological terms.'
>
> *or*
>
> 'The topic of child rearing is clouded in a fog of psychological terms.'

Here are some more examples of mixed metaphors:

> He took the bull by the horns and played his trump card.
> I'd like to be sitting in her shoes.
> I don't mean to step on anyone's sacred cow.
> I've got an ace up my nose.
> That's the pot calling the kettle's bluff.
> That thing was jumping up and down like a sieve.
> They are raising the bar and they want us to jump through it.
> They're up the creek without a leg to stand on.
> You hit the nail on the dot.
> You've got to stick your neck out on a limb sometimes.

technical meaning than 'kind' and 'sort', which are more informal terms. It's best to use all three words with 'this' or 'that' rather than 'these' or 'those'. ☼ **This type of paper is good for newspapers** (*not* **This sort of paper** *or* **This kind of paper**)**. I prefer this type of car** (*not* **I prefer these types of car**)**. He loves that kind of holiday.**

last / past

When you're referring to a time period ending now, use 'past'. When you mean a time period ending at any time before now, use 'last'. ☼ **Over the past week** (meaning in the 7 days before now)**. During the past 5 years** (meaning in the 5 years before now)**. The last days of his life** (where the life ended some time ago)**. In the last months of 2003.**

learnt / learned

In British-English, you can use either 'learnt' or 'learned', although 'learnt' is more common. In American-English, 'learned' is more common. The same applies to dreamt / dreamed, burnt / burned, spelt / spelled, spilt / spilled and spoilt / spoiled.

letters

If you don't know the name of the person you're writing to, put 'Dear Sir', 'Dear Madam' or (if you don't know the sex of the person) 'Dear Sir or Madam'. End the letter with 'Yours faithfully', signing yourself with your initials and surname.

If you're writing a formal letter and you do know the name of the person you're writing to, but haven't spoken to them or met them, end the letter with 'Yours sincerely' (*not* 'Faithfully

yours', 'Sincerely yours', Yours truly' or 'Yours respectfully').
Sign yourself with your first name and surname.

If you're writing a formal letter to someone you feel you can
address by his or her first name, end with 'Yours sincerely',
signing yourself with your first name.

For informal letters, it's fine to write 'Regards', 'Kind regards',
'Best wishes' or 'Yours'.

See also: addresses; Box 10

like / such as

'Like' means 'similar to' or 'same as'. It doesn't mean 'such as'.
☼ **'Products such as honey do well.' This means that honey
is an *example* of products that do well. If it's written as
'Products like honey do well', this means that products
similar to honey (i.e., not necessarily honey itself) do well.**

lists

A sentence introducing a displayed bulleted list ends with a
colon. If you subdivide a list item, use dashes rather than bullet
points. Don't put 'and' before the last item in a bulleted list.

☼   **The main elements of this approach are:**
   • **centre-wide consultation;**
   • **appointment of external consultants;**
   • **involvement of staff through:**
      – **field visits**
      – **data collection.**

You'll notice in the list above that each line ends with a
semi-colon. It's fine to do this, but it's becoming common
now not to use semi-colons at the end of list items. If you look

through this book, you'll see that this is the approach that we use. Note, however, that we still put a full stop after the last item in the list. Some people prefer not to do this; this is fine, as long as it's applied consistently.

✺ **The main elements of this approach are:**
- **centre-wide consultation**
- **appointment of external consultants**
- **involvement of staff.**

In lists that are embedded in the text, you need to use semi-colons and to put 'and' before the last item in the list.
✺ **The main elements of this approach are: centre-wide consultation; appointment of external consultants; and involvement of staff.**

If the elements in a list need to be numbered for ease of reference elsewhere in the text, use numerals (preferably roman) and, if further subdivision is necessary, letters.

✺ **The main elements of this approach are:**
- **(i)   centre-wide consultation**
- **(ii)   appointment of external consultants**
- **(iii) involvement of staff through:**
  - **(a) field visits**
  - **(b) data collection.**

Alternatively, in the above example you could replace (i), (ii) and (iii) with 1, 2 and 3, and (a) and (b) with 3.1 and 3.2.

See also: alphabetical order; bibliographies and reference lists; colon; etc.; semi-colons

long term / short term

Use these phrases only if it's clear from the context what the time span is. Remember to use a hyphen if the phrase is used as an adjective. ☼ **Over the next 3 to 5 years the market for copper will expand, but in the long term it is likely to decline. The short-term outlook for her recovery is not good.**

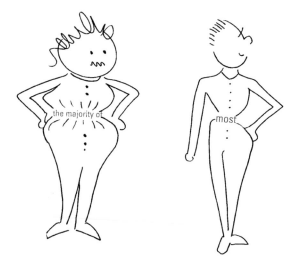

lots of / a lot of

These are common phrases in spoken English, but try to avoid them in formal written English. Use 'many', 'a great deal', 'much' or 'a large number of' instead. ☼ **They did a great deal of work on it (*not* They did lots of work on it). Many people arrived (*not* A lot of people arrived).**

majority / most

When you're referring to a single item, don't use 'majority'. ☼ **Most of the money (*not* The majority of the money).** Use 'majority' only when you're referring to a number or group of items. In most cases, however, it's better to use 'most'. ☼ **The majority of books / Most books. The majority of farms / Most farms.**

may / might

'May' is used when permission to do something is being asked or granted. 'Might' is used to indicate possibility. Take care not confuse them with 'can' or 'could', which refer to the ability to do something. ☼ **May I have some more tea? (***not* **Can I have some more tea?** *or* **Might I have some more tea?) If he doesn't leave soon, he might miss the meeting (***not* **If he doesn't leave soon, he could miss the meeting).**

measurements

Use metric measurements where possible. ☼ **Celsius (***not* **Fahrenheit), hectare (***not* **acre), kilogram (***not* **lb or pound), litre (***not* **gallon), tonne (***not* **ton).**

Note that calibre is a measurement of size, not mass. So a gun cannot be 'heavy calibre' or 'light calibre'. It has a 'large calibre' or a 'small calibre'. Similarly, temperatures cannot be hot or cold, only high and low. Also, prices cannot be cheap or expensive, only high and low. ☼ **Her temperature was high (***not* **Her temperature was hot). The market price was low (***not* **The market price was cheap).**

See also: abbreviations and contractions; Box 13; numbers; per

media

'Media' is plural and so it's followed by a plural verb. ☼ **The media were split on the issue (***not* **The media was split on the issue). The media have covered the story well (***not* **The media has covered the story well).**

Box 12   WRONG WORDS

People often write words that seem, sound or look like the right word, but aren't. Sometimes, the chosen word means quite the opposite of what the writer intends. Here are some common culprits.

AFFECT / EFFECT: 'Affect' means 'influence' or 'pretend'. 'Effect', used as a verb, means 'bring about' or 'cause'. When you use 'effect' as a noun, it means 'result' or 'consequence'. ☼ **The changes affected her work. She affected concern, but she wasn't interested. He effected important changes. The effect of the changes was greater efficiency.**

AGGRAVATE / IRRITATE: 'Aggravate' is often used, incorrectly, to mean 'annoy' or 'irritate'. It means 'make worse'. ☼ **The problems were aggravated by low staff morale. His poor time-keeping irritated her.**

ANTICIPATE / EXPECT: 'Anticipate' means 'foresee' or 'prepare for' something. It doesn't have the same meaning as 'expect'. ☼ **He anticipated his opponent's intention and moved out of the way. I anticipated the comedian's punchline. We expected to find some good books.**

APPRAISE / APPRISE: 'Appraise' means 'estimate the value' of something. 'Apprise' means 'inform'. ☼ **He appraised the paintings for insurance purposes. I apprised him of the details of the contract.**

ASCRIBE / SUBSCRIBE: 'Ascribe' means 'attribute to'. 'Subscribe' means 'follow' or 'pay for'. ☼ **He ascribed his success to hard work. He subscribed to the idea that hard work leads to success. She subscribed to the magazine.**

AVOID / PREVENT: 'Avoid' means 'go round' or 'keep away from'. Prevent means 'stop happening'. ☼ **They avoided each other at the meeting. A last-minute agreement prevented strike action.**

CLASSIC / CLASSICAL: 'Classic' describes things that are outstanding examples of their kind. 'Classical' refers to (i) things from ancient Greece, Rome or similar ancient civilisations and (ii) formal concert music written by such composers as Beethoven and Mozart. ☼ **The Derby Bentley is a classic car. He made the classic blunder of arguing with the traffic warden. The museum displayed many classical vases. She had dozens of classical music CDs, but only a few jazz ones.**

COMPLEMENTARY /COMPLIMENTARY: 'Complementary' means 'matching' or 'corresponding'. 'Complimentary' means 'free', 'on the house', 'flattering' or 'congratulatory'. ☼ They were dressed in complementary autumn colours, she in yellow, he in orange. The hotel offers a complimentary breakfast. He was complimentary about her report.

CONTINUOUS / CONTINUAL: Use 'continuous' when you're describing an uninterrupted process. Use 'continual' when a break in the process is implied, and you mean 'recurring' or 'repeated'. ☼ There was a continuous improvement in sales over the year. They had continual problems with the new software.

CONVINCE / PERSUADE: 'Convince' means changing someone's beliefs or opinions, and is usually followed by 'that' or 'of'. 'Persuade' means spurring someone into action, and is usually followed by 'to'. ☼ I convinced him that the report had to be rewritten. I persuaded him to put the report in the bin and start again.

DECEPTIVE / DECEITFUL: 'Deceptive' means 'misleading'. 'Deceitful' carries the stronger suggestion of 'deliberately lying' or 'being untruthful'. ☼ The regulations sought to stop them making deceptive statements. It is deceitful to claim that you are younger than you really are.

DEFUSE / DIFFUSE: 'Defuse' means 'disarm' or 'pacify' (literally, 'remove the fuse'). 'Diffuse' means 'spread out' or 'scatter'. ☼ They defused a tense situation through quiet negotiation. The odour diffused slowly throughout the house.

DEPENDANT / DEPENDENT: 'Dependant' is a noun, meaning someone who depends on someone else. 'Dependent' is an adjective. ☼ The woman had three dependants, her two children and an aunt. The seaside holiday business is dependent on good summer weather.

DISCREET / DISCRETE: 'Discreet' means 'judicious', 'tactful' or 'keeping a secret'. 'Discrete' means 'separate' or 'not attached to'. ☼ This information is potentially embarrassing, so do be discreet. Gases consist of discrete molecules.

DISINTERESTED / UNINTERESTED: 'Disinterested' means 'impartial', 'neutral' or 'unbiased'. 'Uninterested' means 'not interested'. ☼ We need a disinterested party to mediate in the dispute. He's uninterested in anything to do with cars.

DRAMATIC / DRASTIC: 'Dramatic' means 'significant' or 'remarkable' and can have positive or negative associations. 'Drastic' means 'severe' and generally has negative associations. ☼ **After the training, there was a dramatic improvement in her performance. Poor planning had drastic results.**

ECONOMIC / ECONOMICAL: 'Economic' means 'profitable' or 'relating to economics'. 'Economical' means being careful with resources. ☼ **It is more economic to make the toys in China. From an economic perspective, the country was in trouble. With a reduction in the grant, the charity had to be more economical.**

ENORMITY / ENORMOUSNESS: 'Enormity' refers to things that are outrageous, often in the sense of 'evil' or 'crossing moral boundaries'. 'Enormousness' refers to size, usually meaning 'immensity'. ☼ **It was only when the troops entered Belsen that they realised the enormity of Hitler's crime. The enormousness of the sculpture was not apparent until you got close to it.**

EQUABLE / EQUITABLE: 'Equable' means 'moderate', 'calm' or 'even-tempered'. 'Equitable' means 'fair' or 'just'. ☼ **Her untidiness would upset the most equable person. The contract terms seemed equitable.**

ESPECIALLY / SPECIALLY: 'Especially' means 'above all', 'chiefly' or 'particularly'. 'Specially' means 'solely' or 'for a specific purpose'. ☼ **They looked through all the reports, especially the most recent ones. He was especially keen to expand the gift section. She flew to Geneva specially to see the head of the organisation.**

GRAND / GRANDIOSE: 'Grand' means 'majestic', 'splendid' or 'imposing'. 'Grandiose' suggests pretentiousness, affectation or pompousness. ☼ **The new bridge spanning the River Severn is a grand structure. The hotel lobby, with its crystal chandeliers, marble columns and monumental staircase guarded by life-size granite lions, was rather grandiose.**

HOMOGENEOUS / HOMOGENOUS: 'Homogeneous' means 'the same kind' or 'uniform in composition'. 'Homogenous' means 'similar through common descent'; it's usually used only in biology. ☼ **The people in forest areas are a fairly homogeneous group. The party is not homogeneous; there are many shades of opinion. The forelimbs of fish are homogenous.**

INCREDULOUS / INCREDIBLE: 'Incredulous' means 'disbelieving' or 'showing disbelief'. 'Incredible' means 'unbelievable', 'improbable' or 'beyond belief'. ☼ She was incredulous at the news of inheriting such a large sum. It's incredible that he was able to walk after the accident.

LABOUR / BELABOUR: 'Belabour' means 'beat', 'pound' or 'chastise'. When referring to talking about something in tiresome detail, use 'labour', not 'belabour'. ☼ The guards belaboured him until he stopped struggling. The manager belaboured his staff for their poor performance. He laboured the point until we could stand no more and walked out.

MILITATE / MITIGATE: 'Militate' means 'have a strong effect on' and is usually followed by 'against'. 'Mitigate' means 'reduce the effect of' and is not followed by 'against'. ☼ His offhand manner militated against good working relationships. He is sorry, but this does not mitigate his treatment of the staff. The effect of the cancellation was mitigated by the offer of extra air miles.

OFFICIAL / OFFICIOUS: 'Official' relates to authority, whereas 'officious' relates to applying rules and regulations too strictly or in an overbearing way. ☼ The tenants received official notice of the rent increase. They will fight any officious action that threatens to delay the project.

PRESCRIBE / PROSCRIBE: 'Prescribe' means to 'recommend' or 'authorise' something. 'Proscribe' means to 'ban' something. ☼ The doctor prescribed antibiotics. Her boss prescribed a long holiday. Smoking in the office is proscribed. Sexist comments are proscribed.

PRINCIPAL / PRINCIPLE: 'Principal' means 'main', 'most important' or 'head' of something. 'Principle' refers to values and beliefs. ☼ The principal reason for the move is not clear. The strategy is based on the principle that customers come first.

SYSTEMIC / SYSTEMATIC: 'Systemic' relates to a whole system. 'Systematic' means 'methodical' or 'following a set system or method'. ☼ The tendency to use jargon was systemic in the company. Solving the murder required sifting through the evidence systematically.

TENET / TENANT: A 'tenant' rents property. A 'tenet' is a 'belief' or 'precept'. ☼ New tenants have moved into the offices. Underlying his argument was the tenet that protectionism should be phased out.

71

mid-

When attached to a noun or another adjective, 'mid' always has a hyphen. ✻ **mid-1990s, mid-term, mid-Victorian.**

more than / less than

Use 'more than' rather than 'over' or 'above' when you're referring to an amount or a number of something. ✻ **There were more than 50 people there (*not* There were over 50 people there *or* There were above 50 people there).**

Similarly, use 'less than' rather than 'under'. ✻ **It was less than a mile to the hotel (*not* It was under a mile to the hotel).**

See also: fewer / less

names of people

When you first mention someone's name in a document, use the full name (without the title); thereafter, use only the surname, with or without a title. ✻ **Among the new books is *Evaluating Information* by Donald Monro. An expert in evaluation, Dr Monro focuses mainly on radio (*or* An expert in evaluation, Monro focuses mainly on radio).**

In most business documents, avoid using someone's first name only. Don't use a diminutive (e.g., Pat for Patricia, or Tony for Anthony) unless the person prefers this.

Don't use a mixture of full names and initials unless the person prefers this or it's common usage. ✻ **John F. Kennedy (*not* John Kennedy).** Similarly, use people's middle name, not their first name, if that's what they prefer. ✻ **Rupert (*not* Keith, his first name) Murdoch.**

Box 13   SHORT MEASURES

Here are the standard abbreviations for some common units of measurement.

UNIT	ABBREVIATION
byte	B
carat	ct
Celsius	C
centimetre	cm
gram	g
gigabyte	GB
hour	h
hectare	ha
kilobyte	KB
kilogram	kg
kilolitre	kl
kilometre	km
kilometres per hour	kph
kilowatt	kW
litre	l
metre	m
megabyte	MB
miles per hour	mph
milligram	mg
millimetre	mm
minute	min
second	sec
tonne	t
watt	W

Where names include 'de', 'de la', 'du', 'van', 'mac', 'mc', 'van dem', 'von', and so on, ensure that you use lower and upper case correctly. (For more on lower and upper case *see* capital letters.) Don't omit the accents in foreign names. With some

73

foreign names (e.g., Chinese), the surname precedes the first name; if you're not which is which, it's better to put the name down in full than to guess.

Take care to use people's correct titles. Don't call someone 'Mr' if he is a 'Dr'. Use 'Ms' if you're not sure whether someone is 'Miss' or 'Mrs'.

See also: abbreviations and contractions; apostrophe; bibliographies and reference lists; capital letters; letters

names of places

Put the names of cities in their English form. ☼ **Brussels (***not* **Bruxelles), Munich (***not* **München), Florence (***not* **Firenze), Geneva (***not* **Genève), Vienna (***not* **Wien).**

See also: capital letters; comma; countries and regions

This is followed by a singular verb. Think of it as short for 'no one' or 'not one'. ☼ **None of them has arrived (***not* **None of them have arrived). None of the applicants is suitable (***not* **None of the applicants are suitable).**

not only...but also

Take care where you put 'not only'. ☼ **The meaning of 'The managers read not only *Catering Weekly* but also...' is not the same as 'The managers not only read *Catering Weekly* but also...'.** The first one implies that *Catering Weekly* was not the only publication they read; the second one implies that they did other things with *Catering Weekly* apart from reading it.

Always use 'not only' with 'but also' or 'also'. ☼ **The manager read not only *Catering Weekly*, but also *Hotels and Restaurants*. The manager not only read *Catering Weekly*, she also used it in training workshops.**

numbers

Spell out numbers from one to nine unless they precede a measurement (distance, time, weight, etc.). From the number 10 upwards, put numerals, except where you're using them in an inexact or colloquial sense or at the start of a sentence or as part of a word. Put a hyphen between words that make up a number. ☼ **eight students, 78 countries, 2 years, 5 km. About a hundred people came. I have a thousand things to do. Twenty-three people ordered books (*not* 23 people ordered books). There was a tenfold increase in yield.**

Avoid starting a sentence with a year. ☼ **The year 2006 was a year of change** (*not* '2006 was a year of change', although this usage is common in spoken English).

When you're using a number as an adjective, spell it out unless it's part of an official title. ☼ **The sixth country to join was France. A fifth of the participants were from the Ukraine. 3rd Global Trading Workshop.**

Use a short dash (–), not a hyphen, when linking numbers. Drop the first measurement word when linking two measurements. ☼ **16–44 cm, £5–6 million** (*not* 16 cm–44 cm, £5 million–6 million); **between 60 and 90 km** (*not* between 60 km and 90 km). Don't use a dash when you're putting 'from' or 'between' before numbers. ☼ **from 16 to 44 cm** (*not* from 16–44 cm); **between 80 and 100 people** (*not* between 80–100 people).

For numbers containing four or more numerals, put a comma after each set of three numerals, working from the right (except for years). ☼ **2,376; 100,000; 1,345,789; the year 2004.** Simplify long numbers where possible. ☼ **1.5 billion** (*not* 1,500 million), **3 million** (*not* 3,000,000).

Hyphenate numbers and fractions when they're spelt out. When using numerals, avoid fractions if possible; use decimals instead. ☼ **Thirty-five, two-thirds, three-quarters, 3.5 mm.**

See also: abbreviations and contractions; addresses; amount / number; Appendix 3 under 'page numbering'; Box 4; colon; comma; currencies; hyphens and dashes; more than / less than; superscript

of

Phrases such as 'bored of', 'could of' and 'fed up of' – now common (but incorrect) in spoken English – are creeping into written English. Don't use them. ☼ **I'm bored with this magazine** (*not* I'm bored of this magazine). **He could have** arrived on time (*not* He could of arrived on time). I'm fed up with this job (*not* I'm fed up of this job).

only / just / mainly / entirely

Where possible, use 'only' rather than 'just'. ☼ **There's only one travel agent left** (*not* There's just one travel agent left).

'Only', 'mainly' and 'entirely' are often placed incorrectly. They should come immediately before the word or phrase they are qualifying. ☼ **He went to the market only once** (*not* He only went to the market once). **She had only one report** (*not* She only had one report). **The loss is due mainly to the exchange rate** (*not* The loss is mainly due to the exchange rate). **The damage was caused entirely by the wind** (*not* The damage was entirely caused by the wind).

See also: Box 14

Box 14   IF ONLY...

The meaning of a sentence containing the word 'only' varies according to where 'only' is placed.

SENTENCE	THIS IMPLIES THAT...
Only the daughter praised her brother.	*No one else praised him.*
The only daughter praised her brother.	*She had no sisters.*
The daughter only praised her brother.	*She never found fault with her brother.*
The daughter praised only her brother.	*She didn't praise anyone else.*
The daughter praised her only brother.	*She had no other brothers.*

onto / on to

Use 'on to' when the meaning implies moving towards
something. Otherwise, use 'onto'. ☼ **She walked on to the
stream** (*not* **She walked onto the stream**). **Put the box onto
the pile** (*not* **Put the box on to the pile**). **He fell onto the
safety net. We've added a room onto the house.**

paragraphs

Avoid using one-sentence paragraphs unless the sentence is
fairly long or you want a punchy effect. Otherwise, there are
no general rules about paragraph lengths.

See also: Appendix 2; Appendix 3; Box 10; hyphens and dashes

per

Use 'per' rather than a slash or oblique (/), except for exact
measurements. ☼ **The annual cost is only a few euros per
head** (*not* **a few euros/head**). **Spread the mixture at the rate
of 20 kg/ha. The import duty on bananas is €75/tonne.**

plus

Using 'plus' is common in spoken English, but don't use it in
formal written English. ☼ **She had several papers to write,
as well as a book to review** (*not* **She had several papers to
write, plus a book to review**).

prepositions
(at, by, in, on, to, with)

Try not to end a sentence with a preposition, but don't garble
language simply to avoid doing so. ☼ **'There is the person**

he spoke to' sounds much better, and less pedantic, than 'There is the person to whom he spoke.' (For more on prepositions *see* Appendix 1.)

In protest against someone's effort to avoid ending sentences with a preposition, Winston Churchill scribbled in the margin of the offending document: "This is English up with which I will not put."

See also: capital letters; either…or / neither…nor

pronouns
(I, you, he, she, it, we, they)

Don't make the common mistake of mixing singular nouns with plural pronouns (such as 'we' and 'they') in a sentence.
☼ **In the sentence 'Ask each woman where they buy sugar', 'woman' is a singular noun and so it should be followed by the singular pronoun ('she'), *not* the plural pronoun ('they'). The sentence should be 'Ask each woman where she buys sugar.'** (For more on nouns and pronouns *see* Appendix 1.)

See also: amid / among / between; collective nouns; countries and regions; I / me / myself; sexist writing

punctuation

Good punctuation makes all the difference between writing that is easy to read and writing that is not, so it's worth trying to get it right.

See also: abbreviations and contractions; accents; acronyms; Appendix 2; apostrophe; bibliographies and reference lists; Box 8; brackets; captions; colon; comma; company names; ellipses; exclamation mark; full stop; hyphens and dashes; lists; per; quotation marks; quotations; semi-colon

Box 15   PROBLEM PLURALS

For the plurals of most nouns you simply add an 's', but for a few nouns this is not the case. Here are some examples.

agendum	agenda
child	children
church	churches
criterion	criteria
datum	data
erratum	errata
foot	feet
formula	formulae
forum	fora
lady	ladies
leaf	leaves
man	men
medium	media
referendum	referenda
tooth	teeth
woman	women

But changes are happening. For example, it's acceptable now to use 'agenda' as a singular noun (as in 'The agenda for today is…') and most people write 'forums' not 'fora'.

Sadly, it's all too common now to see plurals created by adding an apostrophe and an 's'. This is not correct. Common culprits often seen in shop windows are: CD's and DVD's (when it should be CDs and DVDs). (*See* acronyms; apostrophe.)

quantum leap

This phrase is often used to indicate 'a great stride forward'. This is somewhat ironic because a quantum means the smallest possible amount of a given property (notably energy). Perhaps 'quantum leap' derives from the scientifically significant 'leap' of an electron from one level to another. Whatever its origin, it's universally understood now and therefore acceptable in a non-scientific context. But it is a cliché, so is best avoided.

quotation marks

Remember that every opening quotation mark must be followed at some point by a closing quotation mark. Use double quotation marks only for quoted material. If there is a quotation within quoted text, put it between single quotation marks. ☼ **The journalist wrote that "the economy is, in the Chancellor's words, 'going from strength to strength' despite the recession elsewhere in Europe."**

In all other instances, use single quotation marks (e.g., to highlight a word or phrase, for slogans, for straplines and for the titles of meetings, book chapters and journal and magazine articles). ☼ **The term 'social capital' captures the idea of social bonds in society. The campaign slogan was 'Fair trade for all!' The ABTA seminar on 'New routes to southern Europe' took place in June. In *The Project Workout*, the chapter on 'Implementing projects' is particularly good.**

See also: bibliographies and reference lists; commas; italics; quotations

quotations

If you're quoting text from a published source, you should use the exact words of the original (with a few exceptions, as noted in the entries on 'brackets' and 'ellipses').

If the text between quotation marks is a complete sentence, put the full stop before the closing marks. If the text between quotation marks is not a sentence, put the full stop after the closing marks. ☼ **"Much of what passes for evaluation is not useful."** He said that much of what passes for evaluation **"is not useful".**

Put a comma after the last word introducing a full-sentence quotation. ☼ **Dr MacAdam said, "The information kept us aware of the issues."** When you're breaking a quotation in mid-sentence (where there is a natural break) to insert the name of the speaker/writer, put a comma after the name of the speaker/writer. ☼ **"The information kept us aware not only of the issues," said Dr MacAdam, "but also of the people involved."**

The same rules apply when there is more than one quotation in a sentence. ☼ **When I meet students whose grammar is poor, I ask them, "Why?" and they reply, "We were never taught any grammar."**

When you're quoting text that is more than about four lines long in normal type (40–60 words), it's usually best to use a display format (rather than embedding the quotation in the text). When using a display format, indent the quoted text on the left and right, and don't use quotation marks. ☼ **In his book *The Complete Plain Words*, Sir Ernest Gowers wrote:**

> **Correctness is not enough. The words used might all be words approved by the dictionary and used in their right senses; the grammar might be faultless and the idiom above reproach. Yet what is written might still fail to convey a ready and precise meaning to the reader…The basic fault of present-day writing is a tendency to say what one has to say in as complicated a way as possible.**

See also: brackets; colon; copyright; ellipses; quotation marks

Box 16 SPELL-CHECKERS AND DAFT CONTRACTS

You should always proofread your work carefully, reading every word (*see* Appendix 2).

Don't rely on the spell-checker to highlight spelling mistakes. You could end up sending off a document with some embarrassing mistakes that a spell-checker would not have picked up, such as:

The lawyer spent weeks drawing up a daft contract.
Instead of a fortnight in New York he had a wee in Washington.
She took up her new position in pubic affairs.
We have organised some trails of the new system.
The monks were busy making Napoleon bandy.
Pensioners on a low income are finding it hard to exit.

respectively

When you're linking two or more items in a sentence with, in the same order, two or more subsequent items, put 'respectively' after the second instance. ☼ **By-products account for about 46, 38 and 32% of cattle, pig and poultry production, respectively. There were seminars on recruitment and promotion on Monday and Tuesday, respectively.**

self-

When attached to a noun or adjective, 'self' is always followed by a hyphen. ☼ **self-esteem, self-help, self-educated man, self-employed person.**

semi-colon

A semi-colon (;) is longer than a comma, but shorter than a full stop. It links two or more statements that:

- are closely related
- are of more or less equal importance
- can usually (but not always) stand as sentences (or clauses) in their own right.

☼ Red stands for poor performance; blue stands for satisfactory performance; and green stands for good performance. To be born a gentleman is an accident; to die one, an achievement. She fell off the scooter three times; he thought it hysterically funny (*not* She fell off the scooter three times, he thought it hysterically funny). (For more on clauses and sentences *see* Appendix 1 and the page opposite.)

Don't use a semi-colon if the second clause begins with 'although', 'but', 'though' or 'when'. ☼ **He went in early, although he didn't need to** (*not* **He went in early; although he didn't need to). He was about to leave, but then he changed his mind** (*not* **He was about to leave; but then he changed his mind).**

See also: Appendix 2; colon; lists

sentences

The longer a sentence, the less readable and more exposed to misunderstanding it is likely to be. Break long, complex sentences into two or more short sentences. ☼ **The company will not issue a general recall of Tixosan. A preliminary ruling by health officials states that the drug poses no immediate danger to the public** (*not* **The company will not issue a general recall of Tixosan after a preliminary ruling by health officials that the drug poses no immediate danger to the public).**

Use short sentences to break up a series of average-length or long sentences. This creates a rhythm that helps to hold the reader's attention and improves the flow of your writing.

Make sure that the arrangement of words in a sentence (the syntax) doesn't lead to ambiguity. ☼ **The tutorials, in five languages, are designed for individual learning and are free of charge** (*not* **The tutorials are designed for individual learning and are free of charge in five languages).**

And it is perfectly acceptable to start a sentence with 'And'. It is also acceptable to start a sentence with 'But' when a point needs to be emphasised. ☼ **They had been told it would be easy. But this was clearly misleading.**

See also: Appendix 1; Appendix 2; Box 2; Box 8; brackets; captions; comma; ellipses; lists; paragraphs; quotations; semi-colon

sexist writing

If you're in doubt about whether to use 'he' or 'she', don't resort to 'he/she' or 's/he'. Instead, convert the sentence into the plural; this allows you to use the neutral 'they'. ☼ **Pilots should not fly if they are feeling unwell (*not* A pilot should not fly if he is feeling unwell).** Alternatively, avoid the use of pronouns altogether. ☼ **Pilots who are feeling unwell should not fly.** (For more on pronouns *see* Appendix 1.)

Don't assume (or appear to assume) that directors, managers, researchers and surgeons, for example, are 'he' and librarians, secretaries and social workers are 'she'. Use the neutral terms now commonly used instead of sexist terms, even if some of them do seem a bit ugly. (*See* Box 17.)

Avoid using 'man' as a verb. ☼ **The feeding station was staffed all day (*not* The feeding station was manned all day).** Avoid expressions such as 'jobs for the boys' and 'may the best man win'.

Use 'women' rather than 'females' or 'ladies' and don't call adult women 'girls'. ☼ **cleaners (*not* cleaning ladies); saleswomen (when referring specifically to women, *not* salesgirls).** Don't use terms such as 'lady doctors' or 'women lawyers' (you wouldn't call male doctors 'men doctors' or male lawyers 'men lawyers').

shall / will

When you're making a simple statement in the future tense, use 'shall' after the pronouns 'I' and 'we', and use 'will' after 'you', 'he', 'she', 'it' and 'they'. ☼ **I shall talk to the manager. He will come in early tomorrow. Will you come in early too?** If the statement expresses determination or compulsion, however, it is the other way round. You put 'will' after 'I' and 'we', and 'shall' after 'you', 'he', 'she', 'it' and

Box 17   NO SEX PLEASE, WE'RE BRITISH

Many people unwittingly use sexist language, thus reinforcing worn-out old stereotypes. Try to avoid using sexist terms, and find the neutral equivalent term instead.

Here are some examples of common sexist terms and their preferred neutral equivalents.

SEXIST TERM	NEUTRAL TERM
actress	actor
authoress	author
cameraman	camera operator
craftsman	artisan
fireman	firefighter
forefather	ancestor; forebear
Frenchmen	the French
hostess	host
layman	layperson
manageress	manager
man hours	work hours
mankind	humanity; humankind; people
manmade	artificial; manufactured
manpower	staff; labour; workforce
salesman	sales representative
spokesman	spokesperson
the common man	the average person
workmanlike	efficient

'they'. ☼ **I will not tolerate this behaviour. We will persevere. You shall listen! They shall not be allowed to strike.**

In American-English, though, 'shall' is seldom used now, except in a question. ☼ **Shall I prepare the report?** This is also happening in British-English. So if you prefer using 'will', that's fine. That's the approach we have used in this book. Note, however, that 'shall' is still common in legal documents in British-English. (For more on pronouns *see* Appendix 1.)

short words and phrases

Always try to use a short word rather than the equivalent long word. As Winston Churchill wrote, "The best words are the short ones."

Similarly, don't pad out writing with long phrases when one or two words will do.

See also: Appendix 2; Box 6; tautology

spelling

If you're in doubt about how to spell a word, look it up in your dictionary. Don't rely on the spell-checker (*see* Box 16). Where a spelling in a good dictionary (such as the *Shorter Oxford*) differs from the spell-checker version, follow the dictionary version.

When using a spell-checker, make sure that it's set for British-English (*not* American-English) if you're working in a British-English environment. The differences in spelling affect mainly words ending in -ce, -ement, -our and -re.
☼ **offence (*American-English[AE]:* offense), acknowledgement (*AE:* acknowledgment), labour (*AE:* labor), centre (*AE:* center).** (For other common examples, *see* Box 4.)

See also: a / an; -able / -eable / -ible; Appendix 2; Box 16; Box 18; -ise / -ize

split infinitives

It used to be taboo to split an infinitive (the ban was the invention of a pedantic Victorian clergyman). It is now acceptable if the alternative is too cumbersome. ☼ **He is said to greatly admire the monarchy (*not* He is said to admire greatly the monarchy).** (For more on infinitives *see* Appendix 1 under 'verb'.)

Don't split an infinitive with negative words. ☼ **He swore never to work for them again (*not* He swore to never work for them again).**

superscript

Try to avoid using superscript (the small raised letters or numbers that sometimes follow a word). ☼ **15th anniversary (*not* 15th anniversary); No. 3 (*not* N[o] 3).**

Box 18 COMMON MISSPELLINGS

Here are the correct spellings of some commonly misspelt words. Do get into the habit of consulting a dictionary if in doubt about a spelling.

abhorrent
absorption
accelerate
accessory
accidentally
accommodation
acknowledgement
acquaintance
acquire
adjudicator
adviser
advisory
advocate
aegis
aerial
aeroplane
aesthetic
affidavit
affiliate
ageing
aide-de-camp
align
all right
alleged
aluminium
ambience
anaemia
anaesthetic
annihilate
antenatal
aperitif
apparatus
apparent

appreciate
approximate
aquatic
archaeology
arguable
argument
ascend
assign
auxiliary

banister
barbecue
barrister
baulk
benefited
bluish
bookkeeper
breathalyser
brochure
budgeted
bypass

calendar
canapé
cancelled
cappuccino
carousel
caucus
cemetery
censor
centring
channelled
charisma

coalesce
coloration
commemorate
commitment
committee
connoisseur
conscience
conscientious
conscious
contretemps
cordon bleu
counselling
creditworthy

début
definite
delicatessen
desiccate
discoloration
draught

embarrass
encyclopaedia
enroll
enrolment
entourage
entrench
exemption
exercise

focused
foreign
forestall

fulfil
fulfilled
fulfilling
fulfilment

gauge
granddaughter

haemorrhage
harass
heyday
hierarchy
honour
humorous
hypothesis

idiosyncrasy
ineligible
initial
initiative
innocuous
innuendo
install
instalment
investor

jeopardise
jewellery
judicial

liaise
likelihood
liqueur

manoeuvre
mediaeval
meteorology
mileage
millennium
miniature

minuscule
minutiae
miscellaneous
misspell

necessary
negligible
newsprint
no one

officiate
omission
overrun

panacea
pastime
penchant
phoney
polythene
potato
precede
preferable
preferred
prejudice
premises
privilege
psychology

questionnaire
queuing

raconteur
recommend
reconnaissance
recoup
reparable
restaurateur
resuscitate
rhythm
rickety

rigorous
rigour

sceptic
seize
separate
shareholder
sieve
sightseeing
signatory
sizable
sombre
sovereign
stationary (not moving)
stationery (paper, etc.)
storey (as in a building)
subsidiary
successful
successfully
sulphur
supersede
supervisor
swap

tomato
tranquillity
transatlantic
transferable
transferred
travelled
tyre

vacillate
vicious

wilful
wilfully
withhold
workforce
workplace

91

sure to

It is 'be sure to', not ' be sure and'. ☼ **Be sure to make the booking** (*not* **Be sure and make the booking**).

synergy

The word 'synergy' is popping up everywhere. Used correctly, it refers to the benefits of working together rather than separately. But it's now often used to mean simply 'co-operation' or 'collaboration'. Avoid it; it's so overused and tired that, like most jargon, it drains sentences of their energy.

See also: jargon, metaphors, clichés and hype

tautology

'Tautology' refers to something that is unnecessarily repeated. ☼ **He retreated to his seat** (*not* **'He retreated back to his seat'** because 'retreated' means 'go back', so 'retreated back' means 'go back back'). **It remains a problem. It is still a problem** (*not* **'It still remains a problem'** because 'still' and 'remains' mean the same thing).

There are other examples of tautology that crop up frequently. ☼ **planning** (*not* **advance planning**), **bonus** (*not* **added bonus**), **priority** (*not* **first priority**), **consensus** (*not* **consensus of opinion**), **proximity** (*not* **close proximity**), **finished** (*not* **completely finished**), **result** (*not* **end result**), **refer** (*not* **refer back**), **innovation** (*not* **new innovation**), **record** (*not* **track record**), **gift** (*not* **free gift**).

that / which

Use 'which' when you're adding information about something, but 'that' when you're defining something. Put another way, 'that' and 'which' are used to introduce a clause. If the clause is essential to the meaning of the sentence, use 'that'. If the sentence expresses a complete idea without the clause, use 'which'. Always put a comma before and after a clause beginning with 'which'. ☼ **The workshop was the first one that they attended. The workshop, which was held in June, was the first one that they attended** (*not* **The workshop was the first one which they attended** *or* **The workshop that was held in June was the first one that they attended.**)

Use 'who' not 'that' when referring to people. ☼ **They met people who had come from Spain** (*not* **They met people that had come from Spain**).

there / they're / their

Take care when writing words that sound the same, but have different meanings (e.g., 'there', 'they're', 'their' and 'weir', 'we're', 'where', 'wear'). Making mistakes with such words can be embarrassing. ☼ **A spell-checker would not pick up the mistakes here: 'Their not allowed to where they're old clothes when weir visiting there house near the wear.' This should be: 'They're not allowed to wear their old clothes when we're visiting their house near the weir.'**

try to

It is 'try to', not 'try and'. ☼ **Don't try to do too much** (*not* **Don't try and do too much**).

unique

Unique means the only one. Something is either unique or it is not. It can't be 'almost unique', 'fairly unique', 'rather unique' or 'very unique'.

Box 19 WHAT IS THE WORD FOR A WORD THAT…

Is a set of capital letters representing the name of something and making a word	Acronym (e.g., NATO, OPEC)
Is formed from another word by rearranging the letters	Anagram (e.g., source / course)
Describes two words with opposing meanings	Antonym (e.g., rough / smooth)
Has two opposing meanings	Contranym (e.g., fast, dust, left)
Is derived from someone's name	Eponym (e.g., cardigan / Lord Cardigan)
Has the same pronunciation or spelling (or both) as another word, but a different meaning	Homonym (e.g., berth / birth, fair / fair)
Is pronounced like another word, but has a different meaning and spelling	Homophone (e.g., rain / rein / reign)
Sounds like the meaning of the word	Onomatopoeia (e.g., squash, sizzle)
Describes two contradictory words placed together	Oxymoron (e.g., friendly fire)
Is the same spelt forwards and backwards	Palindrome (e.g., radar, tenet)
Is a fictitious name	Pseudonym (e.g., Lewis Carroll / Charles Dodgson)
Describes two words with the same meaning	Synonym (e.g., short / little)

while / whilst

Use 'while', not 'whilst', which is rather archaic. 'While' refers to something happening at the same time, so don't use it instead of 'whereas', which means 'but' or 'on the other hand'. ☼ **She cleaned the kitchen, while he dusted the bedrooms. She liked tennis, whereas he preferred football (***not* **She liked tennis, while he preferred football).**

who / whom

'Who' is the subject and 'whom' is the object. When you're deciding which one to use, look at the clause that comes after, not before, these words. ☼ **Who will take the minutes? Did you see the person who delivered this? (Here, although 'who' is the object of the clause 'Did you see', it is the subject of the clause 'who delivered this'). The manager, whom we greatly admire, is leaving. (Here, 'whom' is the object of the clause 'we greatly admire whom'). From whom did you receive replies? To whom did you post the letter?** (For more on clauses *see* Appendix 1 under 'verb'.)

The same rule applies to using 'whoever' and 'whomever'. ☼ **I will invite whoever wants to come. (Here, although 'whoever' is the object of the clause 'I will invite', it is the subject of the clause that follows it, 'whoever wants to come'). I will invite whomever you choose. (Here, 'whomever' is the object of the clause that follows it, 'you choose whomever').**

whose / who's

'Whose' relates to owning something, whereas 'who's' is short for 'who is' or 'who has'. ☼ **Whose pen is this? It's not clear whose car arrived first. I wonder who's going to be there. Who's been eating my porridge?**

zero-sum game

This is jargon and should be avoided. It refers to a situation where there can be only one winner; one person winning automatically means defeat for the other person.

See also: jargon, metaphors, clichés and hype

(This information on 'zero-sum game' should have appeared earlier in this book, under the 'jargon' entry. But it would be odd calling this 'an A to Z of good English' if there was no item beginning with 'z'.)

Appendices

Appendix 1

SOME BASIC GRAMMAR

You don't need to learn dozens of grammatical terms to be a good writer, but if you do know some of the basics you'll find it easier to write good English.

'Grammar' means the system of rules describing the use of *words* and how they combine with each other to form *phrases*, *clauses* and *sentences*.

WORDS

Grammar classifies words into eight groups: **nouns, verbs, adjectives, adverbs, pronouns, prepositions, conjunctions and determiners.**

As English evolves, new words can be created and added to four of these groups *(nouns, verbs, adjectives, adverbs)*. Examples of new nouns created in the late 20th century include 'website' and 'internet'; examples of new verbs include 'download' and 'reboot'.

In the other four groups *(pronouns, prepositions, conjunctions, determiners),* the words are fixed; we can't invent and add new words to these groups.

Noun

A NOUN is a 'naming word'. It is the name of a person, animal, place, thing or abstract idea. ☼ **boy, dog, town, mountain, chair, book, scent, pleasure, sadness.** When nouns name specific people, animals, places, things or ideas, they are called PROPER NOUNS and usually start with a capital letter. ☼ **Nicholas, Jennifer, Bambi, London, Atlantic Ocean, Mount Everest, St Paul's Cathedral, Christmas, July, Impressionism.**

Verb

A VERB is a 'doing or being word'. ☼ **am, buy, give, laugh, make, run.** Verbs that need to be followed by a noun or pronoun are called TRANSITIVE VERBS. ☼ **I *am* a nurse. You *are* a good organiser. She *bought* it. He *made* a box.** Verbs that don't need to be followed by a noun or pronoun are called INTRANSITIVE verbs. ☼ **He *laughs.* I *run.*** When a verb is preceded by 'to', it is called an INFINITIVE. ☼ **to be, to buy, to give, to laugh, to make, to run.**

Adjective

An ADJECTIVE is a 'describing word'. ☼ **foolish, new, open, two-storey, untidy.** Adjectives describe nouns. ☼ **The *foolish* thought. The *new* book. The *open* door. A *two-storey* building. An *untidy* room.**

Adverb

An ADVERB is a 'modifying word'. Most adverbs (but not all) end in '-ly'. ☼ **clearly, extremely, quite.** Adverbs can modify a verb. ☼ **She spoke *clearly.*** They can modify an adjective. ☼ **She was *extremely* clear.** And they can modify another adverb. ☼ **She spoke *quite* clearly.**

Pronoun

A PRONOUN is a word that stands for a noun or another pronoun. There are several types of pronouns:

- PERSONAL PRONOUNS
  When a personal pronoun is the subject of a sentence, it's a SUBJECTIVE PERSONAL PRONOUN (*I, you, he, she, it, we, they*). ☼ ***I* walked here. *You* are right. *He* sings**

well. *She* came home. *It* is a good book. *We* saw the film. When a personal pronoun is the object of a sentence, it's an OBJECTIVE PERSONAL PRONOUN (*me, you, him, her, it, us, them*). ☼ He praised *me.* They like *you.* She avoided *it.* He will meet *us* there. She called *them.* When a personal pronoun refers to ownership of a person or thing, it's a POSSESSIVE PERSONAL PRONOUN (*mine, yours, his, hers, its, ours, theirs*). ☼ It is *mine.* This is *yours.* **Ours** is the green one. *Theirs* will arrive tomorrow.

- DEMONSTRATIVE PRONOUNS identify a noun (*that, this, these, those*). ☼ *That* is the book I need. *This* is too big. The customers prefer *these. Those* are what he likes.

- INDEFINITE PRONOUNS refer to identifiable but unspecific people, places or things (*another, any, anybody, anyone, anything, each, everybody, everyone, everything, few, many, nobody, none, several, some, somebody, someone*). ☼ *Anyone* can take part. *Nobody* arrived. *Many* were sent, but *few* came back. There are *several* here.

- INTENSIVE PRONOUNS emphasise a noun or pronoun (*myself, yourself, himself, herself, itself, ourselves, yourselves, themselves*). ☼ I *myself* will not subscribe to that opinion. He *himself* was absent, although he had called the meeting.

- INTERROGATIVE PRONOUNS are used to ask questions (*what, where, which, who, whom*). ☼ *What* will you do? *Where* is the car? *Whom* do you think we should employ?

- REFLEXIVE PRONOUNS refer to the subject of a clause or sentence (*myself, yourself, himself, herself, itself, ourselves, yourselves, themselves*). ☼ The doctor pushed *himself* hard. She looked at *herself* in the mirror. We did it *ourselves.*

- RELATIVE PRONOUNS link one phrase or clause to another (*who, whom, whose, that, where, which, whoever, whomever, whichever*). ☼ **The person *who* wins gets a car. The people *whom* she likes will go. The course was the first one *that* they conducted. The course, *which* was held in May, was good. *Whoever* wins will go. I'll read *whichever* report is ready.**

Preposition

A PREPOSITION is a word (or sometimes a phrase) that indicates a relationship between nouns, pronouns and phrases and other words in a sentence (*across, along, at, beside, between, by, for, in, near, on, out of, under, up to, with*). The relationship usually relates to time, place, direction or amount. ☼ **She walked *across* Fifth Avenue. He came *by* train. She stayed *for* a week. He stood *near* the candles. They walked *down to* the site.**

Conjunction

A CONJUNCTION is a 'joining word' that links words, phrases and clauses. There are several types of conjunctions:

- CO-ORDINATING CONJUNCTIONS are the common linking words (*and, but, for, nor, or, so, yet*). ☼ **We have invited men *and* women. The books arrived, *but* they were damaged. I wanted to arrive on time *so* I left before noon.**

- SUBORDINATING CONJUNCTIONS are used to create a subordinate clause (*after, although, as, because, before, even if, if, in case, in order that, now that, only if, since, though, unless, until, when, whereas, while*). ☼ **We will talk *after* she has gone. The show was good *although* it started late. He loved going there *because* it was peaceful. I'll go to London *even if* the weather is bad.**

- CORRELATIVE CONJUNCTIONS are always in pairs and they link elements of a sentence that are more or less equal (*both…and, not only…but also, either…or, neither…nor, whether…or*). ☼ ***Both*** Smith ***and*** Jones were there. ***Neither*** the church ***nor*** the hall survived. She gave ***not only*** money, ***but also*** her time.

Determiner

A DETERMINER precedes a noun. Determiners include the DEFINITE ARTICLE (*the*), the INDEFINITE ARTICLES (*a, an*), quantifiers (e.g., *few, many, some*), possessive adjectives (*my, your, his, her, its, our, their*) and demonstrative adjectives (*this, that, these, those*). ☼ ***the*** driver, ***an*** umbrella, ***two*** birds, ***many*** people, ***my*** book, ***that*** bus.

PHRASES, CLAUSES AND SENTENCES

Phrase

A PHRASE is a group of grammatically related words that does not include a subject linked to a verb. ☼ **in the night sky, teachers and students, planted a new tree, functions of the machine.** The most common types of phrases are the NOUN PHRASE (a phrase with a noun as its head), the ADJECTIVAL PHRASE (which describes a noun phrase) and the ADVERBIAL PHRASE (which modifies the verb). ☼ **The unusually shy boy spoke extremely quietly.** In this example, the noun phrase is 'The boy', the adjectival phrase is 'unusually shy' and the adverbial phrase is 'extremely quietly'.

Clause

A CLAUSE is a group of grammatically related words that contains a subject and a verb and is joined to the rest of a sentence by a conjunction or semi-colon. ☼ ***The boys***

went to the playground when ***the bell rang.*** In this example, the two clauses are in italics; they are linked by the conjunction 'when'. An INDEPENDENT CLAUSE is a clause that can stand by itself as a sentence. ☼ **The boys went to the playground.** A DEPENDENT CLAUSE cannot stand alone as a sentence. ☼ **when the bell rang.**

Sentence

A SENTENCE is a group of grammatically related words that contains a subject and a verb and stands alone. There are three types of sentences:

- SIMPLE SENTENCES have only one clause. ☼ **The teachers and students sat down. They looked at the programme.**

- COMPOUND SENTENCES have two or more independent clauses, linked by a conjunction or a semi-colon. ☼ **The teachers and students sat down and they looked at the programme. It was not what they had expected; there was no mention of their school.**

- COMPLEX SENTENCES have one or more independent clauses and one or more dependent clauses. ☼ **When the students were ready, he handed out the notes, but he didn't have enough copies.** In this example, the independent clause is 'he handed out the notes'; the dependent clauses are 'when the teachers and students were ready' and 'but he didn't have enough copies'.

Appendix 2

TEN TIPS ON WRITING A DOCUMENT

1   The most important questions you should ask yourself
    before you start writing are:

    • What are you writing? (FORM – e.g., advertisement,
      article, letter, report)
    • Who will read your writing? (READERSHIP – e.g., internal,
      external, experts, general public)
    • Why are you writing? (GOAL – e.g., to entertain, impress,
      inform, persuade).

    The answers to these questions will dictate how you
    should write the piece in terms of: *content* (e.g., what
    information should be included and what should not);
    structure (e.g., an established format, or a chronological,
    thematic or cyclical structure); *style* (e.g., formal or
    informal); *words* (e.g., technical or not); *length* (e.g., a set
    length or not); and *presentation* (e.g., subheadings or not,
    single- or double-spaced, appendices or not).

2   When you've answered these questions, plan your writing.
    This involves noting the core issue(s) and keywords of the
    piece, listing the main points you want to make and then
    deciding how to group them and in what order to put
    them. Every piece of writing should have a clear beginning,
    middle and end.

3   Always have a dictionary handy. Everyone has 'blind spots'
    when it comes to the exact meaning of words and to
    spellings. Don't rely on the spell-checker.

> ## Box 20   A USEFUL RULE
>
> A reader should never have to read a sentence twice
> to understand its meaning.
>
> Sentences can have several meanings, of course, or different layers
> of meaning, and readers might want to re-read a sentence to explore
> those meanings, but their first reading of the sentence should be a
> smooth one.

4   Once you start writing, ask yourself (as George Orwell
    did in an essay on the English language) the following
    questions before you write each sentence:

    • What am I trying to say?
    • What words will express it?
    • What image or idiom will make it clearer?
    • Is this image fresh enough to have an effect?
    • Could I put it more briefly?
    • Have I said anything that is avoidably ugly?

    This is the basis of creative writing. All writing, whether
    it is a business document or a novel, should be seen as
    creative writing if you want it to stand out from the pack
    and be noticed.

5   Think about these points when you're writing:

    • use an opening line (or two) that will catch the reader's
      attention
    • use the opening paragraph(s) partly to give readers an
      idea of the main points you will cover and in what
      order you will cover them

- try to mix long and short sentences
- break complex sentences into shorter sentences
- it's all right to have one-sentence paragraphs if you need to emphasise something by letting it stand alone
- use words carefully and precisely
- use no more words than are necessary to make your meaning clear
- where one word can replace two or three words, use one word
- where one-syllable words can replace words of two or more syllables, use one-syllable words
- don't use the passive if you can use the active
- keep the use of adjectives to a minimum
- take care with punctuation, especially apostrophes, colons and semi-colons
- use capital letters correctly and sparingly.

6 The English language is at its best when it is at its simplest. It is at its worst when weighed down with jargon and clichés. Avoid jargon and clichés, especially when you're writing for an external audience.

7 When you've written the piece, print off a draft, correct it on paper, insert the corrections on screen and print again. Remember, few people ever get a piece right first time.

8 When you have a tidy draft, don't proofread it on screen. Print it out and read it out aloud. This will show up things you'd never spot otherwise, such as spelling mistakes, parts of the writing that don't flow well, a dull (or no) rhythm, unnecessary words, punctuation mistakes, missing words, awkward sentences, wrong captions and bad word breaks.

9   Don't make a document look dense with text; this could put readers off before they go to the first word. Make the document pleasing to the eye by having enough white space (e.g., good margins, paragraphs of reasonable and varying lengths, and lists if this suits the form of the document).

10 The best way to sharpen your writing skills and improve the way you express your thoughts in writing is to read widely, both fiction and non-fiction. Look at the style of good writing and try to break it down and absorb it. As we've said, the simplest writing is the best writing, but it can be hard to achieve unless you begin to soak up some of the excellent written English around you in books, newspapers and periodicals.

Box 21 FUN WITH THE FOG TEST

Here's an easy way for you to assess how readable your writing is. Try it out on a sample piece of text you've written, about 20 lines long.

STEP 1. *Work out the average sentence length:* Count the number of words in each sentence. Add these numbers together. Divide the total by the number of sentences.

STEP 2. *Work out the percentage of long words:* Count the words with three or more syllables (excluding names of people or places and any words ending with 'ed', such as 'decided' and 'invented'). Divide this number by the total number of words (which you worked out in Step 1). Multiply this number by 100.

STEP 3. *Work out the Fog Index:* Add your number for Step 1 to your number for Step 2. This gives you the Fog Index, scored as follows:

40 or more	Almost unreadable
35–40	Difficult to read, but possibly acceptable if it's a technical document
30–35	Fairly difficult to read, but possibly acceptable if the document deals with a complex subject and is for internal use only
25–30	Fairly easy to read; acceptable for internal use
20–25	Easy to read; good for both internal and external documents
20 or less	Very easy to read; very good for all purposes – you're up there with the best writers!

Appendix 3

SOME TIPS ON LAYING OUT A DOCUMENT

If you have come to page-layout work via computer software packages such as QuarkXPress and Indesign, rather than via the traditional publishing route, it's possible that you are unfamiliar with the standard publishing conventions. For professional-looking documents and effective communication with others involved in the publication process, you should be familiar with these conventions. You should also be familiar with production terms. ☼ **bleed, cast off, descenders, dpi, endmatter, gutter, half-title, imprint page, leading, offprint, ozalids, plotter proofs, print run, recto/verso, registration, rubric, signature, spot colour, widow.** For those of you who are unfamiliar with these terms, a good starting point is Judith Butcher's book (*see* Appendix 4).

Here, we give an outline of some important dos and don'ts when making up the pages of a document for printing, be it a brochure, newsletter, report, manual or book. (The order is not alphabetical; it follows the process of page-layout work.)

The end product

Before setting up the master pages and starting on the layout of any publication, you need to be clear about the end product in as much detail as possible in terms of the intended length, spectrum of fonts to be used, section/page design elements, colour use, spread of illustrations, text paper, cover, binding and ultimate use. All these factors have a bearing on decisions to be made about the layout and during the layout process. Check that there is nothing in the page design that might pose problems for the text you are about to lay out.

Spacing

Set your rules for spacing before starting the layout and then to stick to them. Inconsistent spacing marks the difference between a professional job and an amateur job. When you've done the master pages, and thus fixed such features as text area, margins, gutters (vertical spaces between columns), running heads (title of publication or part of it running across the top of a page) and page numbers, decide on the space you should allow between, for example, rubrics (short headings) and headings, between headings and the first line of text, above subheadings, between subheadings and the first line of text, between illustrations and captions, and between illustrations and text (the runaround).

Lines and fonts

The eye has difficulty taking in the words in a line of text that is longer than about 70 characters, so don't have wider text columns. When using two or more columns on a page, make sure that the text lines are aligned across the columns (use a baseline grid). Check that all text lines, illustrations and captions that fall at the bottom of a page are aligned with each other.

Fonts fall into two main groups:

- Serif fonts. These fonts have curls or lines (serifs) at the ends of letters. Among the most popular serif fonts are Century, Garamond, Times and Palatino.

- Sans serif fonts. These fonts do not have curls and lines at the ends of letters. Popular sans serif fonts include Arial, Avant Garde, Geneva and Helvetica.

Studies show that the serifs on letters help the reader's eye connect the sequence of letters. They also show that the eye has difficulty reading long texts in sans serif fonts. So it's better to use a serif font for long texts. Sans serif fonts are best suited for boxes, tables, captions and websites. In this book, we have used a serif font called ElegaGaramond for the main text and a sans serif font called Univers for the boxes.

Order

For publications that include a range of items before the main text, such as a contents list, a foreword and acknowledgements, the order in which they usually appear is:

(i)   title page
(ii)   imprint page (with information on copyright, the publisher, etc.)
(iii)   contents list
(iv)   foreword
(v)   preface
(vi)   acknowledgements.

This is followed by:

(vii)   main text
(viii) endmatter (including appendices, glossary, bibliography, acronyms, index).

The items (i) to (vi) are known collectively as the 'prelims' (preliminary matter).

Page numbering

Always start the pagination on the right-hand (recto) page. Thus, recto pages always carry odd numbers and verso (left-hand) pages carry even numbers. The prelims should be paginated in lower case roman numerals (i, ii, iii, iv, etc.). From the first page of the main text onwards, use arabic numerals (1, 2, 3, 4, etc.).

Starting the layout

Don't start page-layout work until the text to be laid in is in its final edited form – every 't' crossed, every 'i' dotted. Altering text once the layout has started not only means work duplication, but also almost invariably leads to error. Minor alterations (e.g., correcting a spelling mistake) that don't affect the way the lines fall on a page can be done at the proofreading stage, but there should be no alterations more substantial than this.

Editing text in layout

If you're doing the layout but are not the text editor, ensure that all text changes at the layout stage are overseen by the text editor. Such changes will always be necessary if the layout is to look professional. A common temptation for people doing page layout is to use various strategies to force the text into set spaces. These strategies include 'tracking' (vertically squeezing letters and the spaces between them), reducing leading (pronounced 'ledding'; the horizontal space in which a line of text lies), changing set margins or even cutting out sentences to make the text fit on the page. Such strategies spoil the look and content of the page. It is better to work with the editor to re-word the text so that the lines fall as they should.

Headings

Headings are ranked A (e.g., title of a report or article), B (e.g., text heading), C (e.g., text subheading) and D (e.g., text sub-subheading), etc. Make sure that the size, placement and use of bold/italic/plain reflects this hierarchy. Higher-rank headings should be in a larger type size than lower-rank headings. It's best not to have more than four ranks of subheadings; a text with too many subheadings is likely to confuse the reader.

Drop caps

This typographical device is often used for the first letter at the start an article, paper, chapter, etc. The drop is usually a two- or three-line one. Take care that the space between the drop cap and the second letter is not too small or too large and that it is consistent throughout the publication. The word (or two) after the drop cap should be in small caps.

T HIS TYPOGRAPHICAL device is often used for the first letter at the start an article, paper, chapter, etc. The drop is usually a two- or three-line one. The word (or two) after the drop cap should be in small caps.

Justified / unjustified text

In unjustified text (a ragged right edge, as in this book) you should have no word breaks at the end of text lines unless absolutely necessary. In justified text (a straight right edge), word breaks (*see opposite page*) at the end of the lines are necessary, but don't have more than three lines in a row ending with a word break.

When you're using justified text, make sure the spacing between words looks all right; often, justified text in narrow columns is afflicted by large white spaces between words. Ways of dealing with this include getting the text editor to edit the text a little (re-write it) or slightly

changing the size of a nearby illustration if there is one.
Also check for 'rivers' (random tracks of white running
down a printed page, caused by poor word spacing).

Paragraph indentation

Don't indent the first line of a paragraph that comes
immediately after a heading or subheading (a common
mistake). If, to denote paragraphs, you're using paragraph
indentation rather than line spaces between paragraphs,
indent the first line of the second and subsequent
paragraphs after a heading or subheading. But if you're
using line spaces between paragraphs, there's no need to
indent the first lines of any paragraphs.

Orphans and widows

The first line of a new paragraph should not fall at the
bottom of a page (orphan); there should always be at least
two lines of text at the bottom of a page. The last line of a
paragraph should not fall at the top of a new page (widow);
there should be at least two lines at the top of a page.
Don't end a page with a colon that is introducing a list or
displayed text.

Word breaks

With justified text it is often necessary to break words at
the end of a line, using a hyphen. Words should be broken
between syllables. Don't break one-syllable or short words
that have no obvious division (e.g., beauty, through, cause,
break, area, title, money, again). Don't divide letters in a
word that are pronounced as one letter, such as 'ph' and
'ch'. ✻ **atmos-phere, tech-nology (*not* atmosp-here,
tec-hnology).**

Try to have at least three letters before and after a word break; avoid, for example, breaking words ending in 'ed' or 'er'. ☼ **traded, farmer** (*not* trad-ed, farm-er). If you do need to separate two letters from the rest of a word, do it instead at the start of the word if appropriate. ☼ **en-courage, de-volve** (*not* encoura-ge, devol-ve).

Break compound words where it's obvious. ☼ **tele-vision, trans-port** (*not* tel-evision, tran-sport). But don't do this if it's likely to lead to mispronunciation or misunderstanding. ☼ **dem-ocracy** (*not* demo-cracy); **exact-ing** (*not* ex-acting); **re-adjust** (*not* read-just). Insert word breaks before '-ing', except where '-ing' is preceded by a double consonant. ☼ **farm-ing, proces-sing** (*not* far-ming, process-ing).

Don't break abbreviations, dates or numbers (even long ones) and don't separate numbers from their units of measurement. ☼ **If a line ends with '500' and the next line starts with 'km', get the text editor to re-write the line so that '500 km' stays together.** Don't break names of people and places and don't end a page with a word break.

Box 22   BREAKING WORDS

When you're breaking a word at the end of a line, make sure that the break is in the right place. Here are some examples.

admit-ting	farm-ing	prob-lem
carry-ing	finan-cier	proces-sing
chil-dren	founda-tion	re-appear
dem-ocracy	help-ful	ship-ping
dis-interest	in-spire	splend-our
divid-ing	insti-gate	table-spoon
drink-able	laud-able	tele-vision
en-titled	moun-tain	trans-port
exact-ing	occur-ring	trick-ling
exces-sive	preju-dice	un-prepared

Tables

Put clarity before gimmickry. Check that all the numbers add up and are consistently aligned (on the left or according to decimal points, etc.). Use a consistent treatment for table and column headings (e.g., in terms of the use of capital letters, bold and italic). Align column headings across the table from the bottom up, not top down. Arrange the items in the main left-hand column alphabetically if possible. Align the notes beneath a table to the left and put them in a smaller type size. Here's an example.

TABLE 10: Main fruit exports from Samoa, 2006 (in tonnes)

Area	Citrus	Durian	Papaya, litchis and guavas	Plums	Passion fruit
Atu	14.3	56.8	47.2	8.6	6.9
Menna	5.6	42.3	51.3	–	7.2
Paken	11.1	23.3	52.4	2.5	–
Yepu	2.4	20.4	12.4	–	3.5
Total	33.4	142.8	163.3	11.1	17.6

Source: Ministry of Agriculture, Samoa

Illustrations

The main elements in illustrations (photos, line drawings, charts, graphs, etc.) should face the centre of a publication. For example, in a photo of a person looking towards an object, that person's line of vision should face the centre of a newsletter, not its outer edges (a common mistake). If you need to flip a photo horizontally, check that there is nothing in the photo to prevent this (e.g., words on paper or a screen that will read backwards if the photo is flipped).

Unless illustrations are self-explanatory or are being used purely as fillers, you should give them a caption. Make sure that all illustrations are credited and that the format of the credit is consistent. (*See* captions.)

When using computer software to alter photos in any way (doing cut-outs, deleting items, enhancing colour, etc.), make sure that you have copyright permission to do this and that it is done carefully.

Always do a thumbnail sketch of a publication once you've completed the layout to give you an overall view of number and placement of illustrations. Are most of them sitting in the bottom right-hand corner of recto pages instead of being evenly spread? Are there too many in the first half of the document and unintentionally few in the second half?

When you're displaying several photos overlapping each other (a montage), the one that is lowest (in a vertical format) and the one that is nearest the outer edge of the page (in a horizontal format) should be in front.

Proof marks

You should be familiar with the conventional proof marks so that there is no error in interpreting proof corrections when proofs of the laid-out document are exchanged. Judith Butcher's book and the *Oxford Guide to Style* provide comprehensive lists of proof marks. (*See* Appendix 4.)

Checklist

From the moment you start setting up the master pages, and throughout the page-layout process, you should be building up a checklist of all the points to check later when you're proofing the document before sending it to be photocopied or printed.

Appendix 4

OTHER SOURCES TO CONSULT

The *What Not To Write* guide is intended to give you an idea of what to bear in mind when writing a document. For more in-depth information, we recommend:*

- *Oxford Guide to Style* (formerly *Hart's Rules for Compositors and Readers*) (Oxford University Press).

You should also have the following publications close at hand:

- *Roget's International Thesaurus* (Collins)
- A good dictionary, such as the *Shorter Oxford English Dictionary* or the *Concise Oxford Dictionary* (Oxford University Press).

If it's part of your job to make sure that documents are written in good English or if you're involved in the production of such publications as in-house newsletters, you should add the following books to your workplace shelf:

- *Copy-editing: The Cambridge Handbook for Editors, Authors and Publishers*, by Judith Butcher (Cambridge University Press)
- *Fowler's Modern English Usage* (Oxford University Press)
- *Oxford Guide to Plain English*, by Martin Cutts (Oxford University Press)
- *The Complete Plain Words*, by Sir Ernest Gowers (Penguin)
- *The Handbook of Non-Sexist Writing for Writers, Editors and Speakers,* by Kate Mosse (The Women's Press)
- *The Oxford Dictionary for Writers and Editors* (Oxford University Press).

Useful websites include:

    www.plainenglish.co.uk
    www.tiscali.co.uk
    www.useit.com/papers/webwriting/writing.html
    www.usingenglish.com

* As most these books are regularly revised and updated, we have not cited specific editions and therefore have not followed the normal rules governing the wording of bibliographical references.

Index

This is an index of:

- the entry headings in the A to Z (**in bold**)
- items on which you'll find information under the entry headings.

For example, 'apostrophe' is an entry heading and so it appears in the index as **apostrophe**, with a page number. 'Lower case' is not an entry heading, but there is information about it under the entry headings **abbreviations and contractions, acronyms, capital letters, names of people** and **quotations**. So if you look up 'lower case' in the index, it refers you to these entries.

Notes

We're leaving the next few pages blank for you to jot down notes on items you might not find in this book but would find useful to have at hand. For example, you might want to jot down spellings that you're never quite sure of, or where the apostrophe goes in a word you come across fairly often but isn't in this book.

If you think that some of the notes you've made might be worth telling us about, or if you spot what you think might be gaps in what is covered in this book, then do send an e-mail about them to info@words-at-work.org.uk or via the e-mail facility on our website (www.what-not-to-write.com) and we'll consider including them in the next edition of *What Not To Write*.

Notes